Practical Occultism

Practical Occultism

FROM THE PRIVATE LETTERS OF
WILLIAM Q. JUDGE

Edited by
ARTHUR L. CONGER

THEOSOPHICAL UNIVERSITY PRESS
PASADENA, CALIFORNIA

Theosophical University Press
Pasadena, California 91109
1980

Library of Congress Catalog Card Number 78-63320

Hardcover ISBN 0-911500-29-4
Softcover   ISBN 0-911500-30-8

Manufactured in the United States of America

PREFACE

As co-founder of the Theosophical Society — and successor to its first Head, H. P. Blavatsky — William Q. Judge sacrificed himself to the cause of those Masters whom he served that Their message find a rooting place in the West. There he felt the foundations of an active Universal Brotherhood must be laid for the preservation and growth of future generations.

Not content with spreading the message his constant counsel to all was to "live the life" for only thus could the message be fully understood. He was a living expression of practical occultism. This is apparent nowhere better than in his private correspondence in which he constantly referred the student to fundamental rules of esotericism, firm adherence to which was essential for the would-be disciple.

The letters in this volume were taken from his *Letter-books* and other private files. It was recognized from the start that the editorial problem was one of peculiar difficulty. Not only was the material in many instances almost indecipherable, but the matter of appropriate selection of the main extracts demanded strict discrimination.

The committee which effectively worked on this assignment consisted of Hazel Minot, Grace Frances Knoche, A. Studley Hart, Lawrence Merkel and James A. Long. Kirby Van Mater rendered aid in making available this material from the Archives of the Theosophical Society.

A. L. C.

Covina, California
September, 1949

—————— 1882-1887 ——————

71 Broadway, N. Y.

Wm. B. Shelley, Esq.   Febry. 13, 1882.
Dear Sir:

Yours of 11th at hand and carefully read. May I ask whether in the little package containing Olcotts address I did not put a copy of the By Laws of the Society? I have a distinct recollection of so doing. My reason for asking is that I have received a request for another copy from Rochester and as at present I have but few, will refer to you instead of sending another. Please let me know.

The facts related in your letter about Mrs. Cables are curious, and cannot be explained fully by me because I have not the necessary knowledge. I am exceedingly glad however that she has been the means of you and your friends being turned from the pernicious views which are held by so many estimable Spiritualists, and it will be a cause for greater rejoicing if through her and you and your friends more converts shall be added in Rochester to what is truth.

Mrs. Cables in teaching you as you say 'philosophy afterwards discovered in Isis' etc, without actual knowledge on her part of that book, was simply telling the truth, which being always around us and to be found, was hit upon by her. *Why* she fell into that current I cannot explain; for it would take a knowledge of causes which I do not possess to give the reasons. The more pure minded any person is, the more free from materiality the more likely is that person to naturally perceive what is the truth.

Many reasons might be adduced for an explanation. First, a natural one that, as I said, she fell so to speak, into the current of truth which ever encircles us, or Second that some adepts had projected those ideas into her mind. But aside from herself 'twould take an adept to determine. Of one thing however I am certain, and that is that the adepts can, if they will, speak through the minds of persons as far away from them even as Rochester. But they do not like to do this except with very pure persons. Perhaps, to touch upon reincarnation, Mrs. Cables's soul may once have made inquiries into this philosophy at an age when it was widely diffused and much cultivated, and now the strong bonds of sympathy assert themselves. I would wish that Rochester and N Y were nearer or that some more rapid means of transit were in use so that we might inquire more deeply into the subject. With the natural powers which you say Mrs Cables has she ought to be able to develope herself much more. I do not mean to develope herself as a medium but to develope the powers, and find out the secrets, of her own soul. She may be doing so and I hope if she is that she may have great success.

When I referred above to the pernicious doctrines held by some Spiritualists, I meant the theory that they communicate with the *Spirits* of the dead, and other theories of like nature, nearly all of which have the effect of belittling the powers of the soul and spirit of the living man,

4

and hardly ever result in anything good. Look for instance at the case of Mrs Cridge-Reynolds who was exposed here the other day. I feel though that you agree with me on these points.

Is it not then my friend the proper time to show the people the path of truth? How much we would be ahead today had the Spiritualists pursued their investigations in the proper manner. Whereas since the Fox rappings in Rochester began nothing at all has been accomplished in the way of real progress.

The Maharajahs of Benares motto is "There is no religion higher than truth," and that is what we seek to find.

Fowler and Wells sell back nos. of Theosophist. I think the numbers you speak of must have been lost. I received mine and so did friends.

Fraternally yours
William Q Judge.

Mar. 8 1882

Mrs. Cables, Rochester.

Madame:

Yours recd at same time with Mr. Shelley's has long stared me in the face. Your "pity for the world and desire to serve and save it and affection for those holy people might attract some intelligence permitting you to serve them." This is no doubt the case. But as for the Brothers and what they are doing and wish to do here, I would be unable to tell you for they do not proclaim their intentions. Their greatest virtue I know is love for humanity and their grand object is the amelioration of the condition of the race. Therefore any one with a similar object and thinking on them must eventually attract their attention altho' that person may not become aware of it. In the Occult World by Sinnett now in print by Colby and Rich are letters from one of the brothers and those letters are full of instruction. Excuse brevity.

Truly yours

WILLIAM Q JUDGE.

------

71 Broadway
E. W. D. Allen   Mar. 14, 1882.
    Rochester, N. Y.
Dear Sir or Madame:

Your handwriting is that of a woman, but as yours of 2^d has no other clue to your sex, I thus address you.

I take a short opportunity to reply begging to inform you that just now I have not the time at my command to devote to a full and complete reply. As I am about to undertake a long journey I cannot spare many minutes from business.

Your remarks submitted with your letter, upon Theosophy, are beyond question the words of a medium under the control of either an outside intelligence; or uttering or writing while in an ecstatic state the ideas of his or her own soul. The name attached was well chosen, and cannot with any show of reason be claimed as the real name of any person, unless it might be that of some friend now dead. It is the name of an ancient Greek Goddess, who "from originally being the personification of the serene bright upper sky, had as early as the time of the epic poets, changed or advanced so as to embody under the divine form a conception of the clear insight of the human mind in its various functions." Therefore the name was well chosen. But do not let names deceive you.

Much of what you sent is very good Theosophy, but much still is so mixed up with various things as to present nothing really tangible.

Theosophy is knowledge of God and love of man, and those are both included in your paper. But there is much that is left for explanation. For instance: "whose concentrate purpose reveals the divine power of mind, with sovereigns enthroned upon enchanted isles in cosmic seas." The last member of this sentence is unintelligible in that connection. What it might mean in certain other connections is not relevant. But have you any idea of its meaning?

There is much of the same sort in the paper; and therefore I cannot subscribe to it as a whole as being the Theosophical teachings which I have learned.

Yet as I first said much of it does in a sort of mystical manner reflect many Theosophical ideas.

I would not, if I were you, publish this paper, because as it now stands you would subject yourself to much, and perhaps some just, criticism.

Now I doubt if to yourself is intelligible one sentence — this: "this knowledge . . . enables each pure desire to be inspired by the psychic force, which at once becomes the charioteer of this human power divine." The question would be "how can the psychic force become the charioteer of the human power divine," and further "how can that psychic force inspire a pure desire; that or draw the pure desire into itself by inspiration of it." Or do you think it should be construed the other way and read to mean that pure desires are inspired *into* us by the psychic force.

On the whole it seems that *Athena's* effort is too transcendental in its mere statement for this age and language. It should be in more plain language, and should have many and glaring redundancies pruned off and inconsistencies corrected.

For myself I could never agree that the psychic force should be the charioteer of the human power divine. If the latter is will-power-perfected then *it* must be the charioteer and psychic force the vehicle. Psychic force must be blind in any case considered by itself and it only acts intelligently when directed by Will or Mind. From this position I could not retreat, so that on that one point I should disagree with Athena.

Again I at present cannot explain "the sacramental marriage of the heart with celestial consciousness and the sympathy Divine."

Theosophy teaches that man's will perfected can emulate the phenomena of nature and know all things. It teaches immortality and a belief in spirit, but it does not teach that the spirits of our departed ones return to this vile atmosphere.

It believes it to be our duty to enquire into these things for the purpose of finding out the laws of spirit and matter so that in the end superstition may be eradicated, knowledge prevail and knowledge of such a character that through it "that great orphan, humanity" — as one of the Theosophical higher Adepts calls it — may be benefited and saved. I must conclude here.

Truly yours
WILLIAM Q JUDGE.

———

Paris, May 11, 1884

Dear Olcott,

You are very right in saying that but little may be expected from French T. S. It is a great expense to the Society, all of us here, and the French are not either delicate or considerate. About all you need to do is to give them a plan upon which to prosecute their work. They are wasters of time. Last night at de Pomar's, as usual after Mohini had said a few words, they all got entangled in French and no real work was done. Thurman had the inexpressible cheek to listen to H. P. B.'s explanation of a matter, and then after ten minutes comes out with it himself, asking when he had finished if he had not given a good explanation. M. Wagner got them off on materialization and 'existe ou n'existe pas,' and poor Mohini and I at one o'clock got home near dead.

9

There were two broad-breasted women, décolleté, three who openly expressed admiration of his eyes. Oh, they are awful. You cannot get a serious hearing. It is in this way well enough to have the Duchess offer her home, but that has drawbacks, as there are many who do not wish to go there, I am told. They ought to have a room hired as Society property and thus be independent. Then they have these interminable jealousies and are so touchy. The night Mohini came they acted very inconsiderately. H. P. B. sent a letter to Mme. de Barreau that Mohini could not be used by outsiders, and she and Mme de Morsier are half insulted. You see de Morsier and Mme. de Barreau have old Le Blois in tow, and he wants to pump all he can out of Mohini, Mme. de M. says, 'Le Blois is very important for France,' but when you ask him if he will join the Society or start one in Strasburg, he 'respectfully declines.'

You would not have been pleased with last night's meeting, but the French character is such that I presume no more can be expected. One of the numerous interesting points in the character is the intensity of their ignorance, their 'newness' so to say. Last night Mme. de Morsier came out with a query about Crookes' psychic notes, which I think is five years old, asking about it as his *last* book, and old Thurman rolled off some lengthy phrases on the subject. All of them called it Crookes' *last* book and were about to ask Mohini about it, when T. Child, the correspondent of the *Sun,* said it was about six years old but that *Figaro* had only just heard of it that morning.

Today Mohini has gone to Mme de Barreau's to see Le Blois et al. He is a poor hand at finding his way. I could not go with him, and he is obliged to wear his overcoat in the hot street or be the cause of an enormous crowd. Yet they did not even suggest a cab for him.

You ought to suggest when you come:

(a) a method of carrying on their meetings that shall result in good progress,

(b) that they shall hire a room somewhere to be used for the purpose,

(c) that they take in honorary members who shall each pay some good sum, etc., etc.

I have received some letters from America from inquirers and others who wish to start Branches. One of the letters was to Damodar, who sends it to me. This is a matter needing attention, because there will be several persons in various parts of the U. S. desiring to start Branches, and the question is how to get over the rule that requires each member to be vouched for. Men in Sacramento, for instance, cannot be at this time vouched for.

You do not reply about Marbel and Mrs. Cables. She and Shelley would do as Councillors for the east and Atlantic side, to whom all applications could be sent, and to have power to initiate persons desiring to form Branches.

I do not know what your rule is about this, as I have never got a reply from you or Damodar about it. It would be a good thing to get up a little circular of instructions about forming Branches in distant places of this

Third Section, as for some time there will be many chances to form *uninitiated* Branches. I would suggest that in cases where we do not know any of the applicants, a certificate from the Town Clerk or other officer be requested to be forwarded with the obligation, request for charter, and fees. I would like to see you about this, and hope you will not let it slip. Of course, if we had a little money we could send around Deputies to start Branches. But new Branches ought to be able to send at least one man for initiation to such places as N. Y., Rochester, St Louis, etc.

Another idea. If we could get hold of a sufficient number of the American colony in Paris to start a Society with some of the proper metal in it, I think a little more might be done. Many foreigners would join it. One difficulty here is that the police supervise these affairs and claim the right to say whether or not a Society shall or shall not exist.

Several Russians have called on Madame, and are proposing to join. Among them is Prince Ourossof who lives here, and I believe last night a Russian Countess joined. I did not get her name, although I did receive the fee. What shall I do with this fee?

Now answer all my queries, do.

I think it is time to start a section *of the Society* which adopts all the doctrine of the Masters and shall propagate it: all members of the § [Section] to subscribe to the doctrine. You and H. P. B. to stay out of it.

As ever,
W. Q. JUDGE.

Dear Olcott,

I arrived at the Bar this morning at 8.30 after a very fine passage. We were long getting in, and it was 1 o'clock before we entered the dock. I saw no one at first, but after a while Mr. Tookaram came aboard, and it appeared that he had been waiting for me all the time, although it was mail day and office hours. He was accompanied by a Mr.—— I forget. Several brothers had been waiting, but went away. They gave me garlands and bouquets, with which I paraded through the streets. It is a pretty custom. We went at once to his office, and I am just writing this to catch the mail which goes in half an hour.

He says there has been no trouble at all about the Coulomb affair, that no one minds her or it, and no one has left in consequence of it. There has not been one word said about it in any of the papers, and if I can stop further progress of pamphlets and exposés, it will be all fixed. This I will do at once.

Many branches have expressed a desire that I should stop on my way and address them. I am to stop here some few days to receive visitors and enquirers. Tookaram says that our prospects are rosy, and I hope with Father's help to give them a rousing up on the subject and get them in in numbers. . . .

You will hear by next mail, as by this I can do no more at present. Tookaram sends you his best love and also to Madame Blavatsky and Mohini.

Give my love to them also and to the Arundales, and

excuse me to Madame for not writing. Tell her for Jesus' sake not to give Coulomb the slightest encouragement until we get them out of India. Remember me also to Baboola.

Affectionately yours,

WILLIAM Q. JUDGE.

---

35 Broadway
N. Y. Feb. 5, 1886

My dear Brother Padshah:

I have received from you the Report of the P. S. Socy. For this I am much obliged as I was just then wanting one and despaired of getting it.

And is this the investigator from whom you asked me to get evidence. Why I wouldnt give him the facts of a mere horse stealing case. He has too much perverting ingenuity. All through he shows ignorance and merely a spirit of denial. He had no desire to investigate, but only to prove the absurdity of everything. In my opinion he has not succeeded.

The chief thing in his argument is "differences between witnesses." But for ages that has been called the true test of a witness's value when the differences do not amount to absolute contradiction. He says that Mohini disagrees with Damodar in that M. said the figure *melted away,* while D. said it appeared to go over a tree "*and disappeared.*" I always thought "melting away" and "disappearance" were synonymous terms. And so he goes all through. Then he lies when he says (1) that there was an aperture behind the shrine. There was not. I exam-

14

ined it, had it all torn down and fully exposed what was there. He never examined me. How do you know that I did not leave India to give him a good chance to hang himself on his own rope; (2) that "Mr. Judge an Am. Theos. was there and desired to see the shrine etc. but was not permitted." This is false. I went there with full authority and from the first moment saw all, had all the keys and took complete charge; (3) that the partition in Damodars room was not examined. It *was* examined and no marks were found on it. Besides it was I who put the Shrine in there when we tore down curtain etc. to examine the wall.

If he thinks his analysis of writing is conclusive he is welcome to that.

I have a lot of letters *not* in H. P. B. writing but in writing *similar to my own* that came to me through myself. It proves nothing. You and I know (at least you ought) that an adept does not always write in his own hand but if he uses another person's organs the writing will resemble theirs.

Then as to Massey. I wrote him some letters from London which he said he would think H. P. B. had written if he did not know I had been the writer.

The whole Report is valuable. It will be of use from time to time. It is however defective in that it does not contain *all* the facts nor all the witnesses.

And I shall always remain obliged to you for it.

Believe me to be
as ever fraternally yours,
WILLIAM Q. JUDGE.

P. O. Box 2659
N Y. April 27 1886

Dear Olcott:

I want to write you about an important matter concerning the Board of Control, so that you may be in possession of inside information when the time comes, and this is all confidential and of course I do not call it a charge against anybody, for when I make that it will be done formally and with proofs. This is between you and me, for I know you have only the Cause at heart no matter how much carping critics, selfseekers, may find fault with you, and you ought to know me by this time.

When you created the A B of C [American Board of Control] in 1884 it did not have E. Coues upon it. You added him after. I suggested Cables as secy and Page as Presid^t. They so decided and remained till July '85. Coues came back here highly recommended by you. They met in 1885 while I was here and Coues became Pres^t and Page Secy — Cables remaining a simple member. Certainly the Board's functions are only administrative and Executive — a small copy of the Council. I did not care to be on the Board satisfied to work unceasingly on the lines we so well understand, and satisfied with you, that any dogmas and mystery are dangerous. I could have got on the Board.

Well, in July they passed those absurd resolutions about being censor of the Psychical Socy and Coues was deputed to explain all to the members. This was and is a real nigger in the fence or woodpile and C had an object which the others did not foresee.

16

Buck, Cables, Page, Doubleday and the rest are all right. As good as gold; but if this Coues stays in it — especially at its head, he will wreck the whole movement, by means of dissension, jesuitical practises, phenomenalism and all sorts of folly, as you will see. Personally, I *am convinced he is a jesuit agent and has worked to that end.*

Well, from his return here until I got things in shape here with Gebhard and everything booming in Boston and elsewhere he did absolutely nothing but organize what he calls a Gnostic Branch which has never held a meeting and to which he talks about astral bells, bodies and what not. He wrote to as many members as he could find to join it in all parts.

I didnt mind him at all and got my branch in good order holding meetings, printing books at cheap prices, establishing a library etc etc, when one day comes a telegram to our place of meeting commanding the Aryan Branch to close its doors, admit no one, and listen in the silence for the astral bells — *in the name of K H and H P B.* It was addressed to the Soc'y. Same night he telegraphed to same address to Dr Dean one of the Gnostic Br. the same thing. I saw that and have a copy. He also wrote me personally "You are making too much noise in N Y. Close your doors, listen in the silence for the voice. Admit no one. K. H." Needless to say I am not a fool, and didnt comply.

Judge Higley — a fine man — who had waited 8 mos for his diploma, decided to join in N Y, asked me to see about it. I wrote Coues so that Higley could get his demit from Gnostic. Coues replied to *Higley* in a long letter saying my Branch was dead, dead, dead, and referred me to that letter. I explained to Higley who said *"For the present I will not withdraw."*

Meanwhile my Branch hard at work on the proper lines, eschewing phenomena and preaching Universal Brotherhood and trying to spread Theosophy.

Next, on April 13th, he wrote Parsons and others here "Am coming to N Y on important business for T. S. *There is great dissatisfaction in N Y on the facts regarding* the SO CALLED Aryan Branch. I am coming to organize a new Branch etc etc." He knew then by letter from me our exact condition and all had been duly reported to Page. He (C) then wrote me a letter I was sure not to get demanding that I come to Higley and prove status of A T S, and bring charter, not telling me of the proposed new Branch. I found that out though. It was on the same night as our meeting. I went at 10 p.m. They had already signed application for new N Y Charter and *did* not tell me anything nor any of our members.

I do not object to any new, needed, Branch, but one has hard work to get along as yet here. To get one room rent is horrible.

I protested after to the Board and it is all pending. Parsons joined application as he said to me "to find out what the fellow is after."

I have demanded, privately, from C his resignation from the Board so as to give him a fair chance and shall then ask the Board to consider it, so it may reach India unless they settle it.

He is either a Jesuit, or a self seeking ass.

There is no dissatisfaction here at all, except with him, and when Parsons asked him that night: "What is the matter," he replied, "there is nothing at all the matter; there is no dissatisfaction."

The Cause now has a big start here, but if he goes on in that way it will be wrecked, unless he is dropped from the Board. As a mere member I do not mind him at all.

So much for my side that I can prove. I received a telegram from Baltimore when he was there, addressed to my house, saying: "a woman has again betrayed you. Now you know why the Masters did not cure you in India H. P. B." I *think* this was from C; if not then Mrs. Holloway. It is all damned rot. Mrs. Judge opened that message. . . .

He [C] writes and tells everybody that we must keep all secret; and seems to think that the whole work is astral body business, bells etc etc of that kind. His talk to the women he had that night in Higley's house was disgusting. Not a word of philosophy: all *his* power to see in the astral light, of which I discredit every word. But I said nothing then.

Now don't imagine I have a quarrel with him. I have not. But good sense and good management seem to point to the propriety of getting him out of the Board in some way. You ought to write me in time for July meeting (4th) of the Board your firm views on the line of T. S. work, the proper scope of the Board and its officers' powers and duties and that Branches should have delegates to its meeting. I am perfectly harmonious with the Board. Do not let the Council give separate rights (autonomy) to U. S. If

19

you do you cannot regulate them and the Jesuits will have us. Now Olcott if I am wrong Master will say so. I have lost personality and while I am hard at work here for T. S. I would to god that I were out of the devilish country and in India.

As ever your brother
WILLIAM Q JUDGE

My Branch is called "Aryan Theosophical Society of New York." So in charter. That other name is a misprint and *lapsis plumæ*.

———

P. O. Box 2659, N. Y. April 29 1886

My dear Friend:

No excuse will, I am sure, be needed from me in addressing a few lines to you in your present sad bereavement, not only because you feel that I write out of sympathy, but also because we both saw the light under the same skies in the same country. Your long absence similar to my own from poor Ireland which is at once the despair and the destiny of its rulers, has not removed from us the common tie which should unite those of the same race; and all the more true is this when we know that that race is, in Europe, *sui generis:* a people not cognizant of their isolated position, of their strange peculiarities, of their strange history, of their immense past. Nor have I the least doubt that you and I in the far distant past knew each other well and we engaged in the same pursuits. Aside from any other proofs, I find confirmation in the peculiar sympathy and profound understanding which exists between your son Z—— and myself, although when first we met in 1884, the prospect of any understanding whatever seemed very far distant from possibility.

What I want to speak about is regarding poor X—— and Y——. I do not deem it possible for me to enter into a mother's feelings, but I have been a father from whom a daughter was snatched away in two days while she was in the flower of health.

It seems to me that there are in the present sad circumstances to be found means of finding comfort. If one were able to look with ease into the astral world, of course then one could *see* without the need of argument, just what had happened, how it came about, and what the result is now.

My own opinion I will give you, assuring you that for me it has no defects, and I think it probable that you will be able to find reason in it.

Going back to X——, I believe that the act he committed became so to speak a picture in the place of its commission. It was however, more than a mere picture. It, that is the act, became so to say a living being inhabited by either an elemental or an elementary. Every thought becomes that, its power depending upon its intensity. And in his case the elementary would not be his own but some wandering, gross, elementary. So every one of us each moment creates these living things. Now in X——'s case why should he be held by any one personally directly responsible for the effect of such a picture or rather, extraneous creation. For being out of this plane altogether he can not see nor control these things while we, living beings, are present to the sight to remove doubts and to be proof to others that what they may see in dreams and visions are not what they know us to be. We are so to say, constant protests against the lying or otherwise acting, other self. But if I did not know this and should see what in dreams I took to be X—— I might think it was X—— himself when in fact it would be only the picture which he produced when he passed away. Those cases of suicide where the deceased may have incited to that act are always those of very depraved persons. In the present case I can see nothing to lead me to suppose it was X——. Nothing whatever.

Not even do I think X—— can be said to have incited to it *unconsciously,* for, if the picture seen by Y—— was only that which the *act* of X—— in its performance produced in the astral light then it cannot by the slightest possibility be laid to the door of the boy X——. If so then of course anything which a psychometer may see could be likewise laid at the door of the person who was the cause of the picture. Again when consider the fact that Y——'s dreams were *not* at all like the thing done by X—— we see at once that it was this irresponsible creation which caused – if anything did – the act of Y——. Why if we were to permit ourselves to argue that X—— himself incited Y——, why then of course in every case where a parent or a friend died disgusted with the world by some disease, leaving a child, friend or lover and thinking perhaps that that child friend or lover were better out of the world also, we must also conclude that the one remaining

22

would be incited to die — for you can die voluntarily without knowing it — by the other who has so passed away.

In cases of suicide the dying thought is very strong and makes a strong picture which is totally removed from the control of the person who caused it to be made. How then can we possibly say X—— incited anyone.

These dreams prove nothing. For dreams are caused by many different and slight causes. When I was a boy I saw every night my own Father as a vindictive and bloodthirsty animal who desired to harm me. Yet he was a most kind and devoted parent who loved me dearly and always was with me in everything. Yet the dreams occurred nearly every night for several years.

These things are difficult to explain. But in many cases the explanation lies in some obscure part of the person himself which he does not know about nor anyone else either.

Now, although I believe that in cases of suicide, the person remains a longer time in the state called Kama Loka, yet that there are great differences in that state I fully believe. A very bad, morose, or dissipated person would be in a very different condition from one who suddenly commits the deed while living a good life and being a person of happy disposition and good family.

So here Y—— necessarily is on a plane where while we know he is in Kama Loka we know he is not necessarily in a terrible state. The same differences are observable there as here. Here in life we are just on the plane into which we projected ourselves from the preexisting conditions, and we see around us great variations of state. So

23

there, no matter how we die, there are also great variations arising from this life which is the preexisting condition for that.

No doubt we can in some way influence persons there by our sympathy, strength and aspiration. Such is our duty. And that would lead us to be strong, to hope, to rely on the Supreme Soul of all which knows and feels all things.

Now I sincerely trust that what I have written may be of some service to you. And that you and your family have my sincere sympathy and help you may be, and I know are, sure of.

With my fraternal and eternal friendship

I am to you and yours as ever

WILLIAM Q. JUDGE

P. O. Box 2659

N Y. May 5 1886

Mrs. Robbins,

Madame:

I have yours of the 2^d enclosing subscription to the Path for which, thanks.

To join a Branch of the T. S. and thus declare you are one is to add another to the ranks of a great movement thus increasing power and sympathy. One's next step is to try to comprehend the doctrines and then to theosophise as much as possible your friends and neighbors; not necessarily to convert them into members but to show them what one himself believes to be true. That is the aim of Theosophy for the society was started to try and get people with one accord to find out truth by first cultivating the idea of Universal Brotherhood. In the Path we are trying to point out the road to all sincere thinking people, if studied with care one should gain from it. No one can really be *told* anything; they may be told a thousand times and not being ready do not understand. We must try to understand with the heart, and from within a light will begin to shine which will clear up doubts and darkness.

The real Ski, if that is the one you have, is a splendid man. I have often spoken with him and think his sentiments are noble. However I never judge as to any particular case. His urging you to take the Path is a good thing for I think in it will appear much that will do us all good. Give him my respects, and ask him if he has any words to say to me, for in the past he said many things, and I would like to hear how he is and what he has now to say.

Believe me to be

fraternally yours

WILLIAM Q JUDGE

May 6 1886

Dear Page:

Yours rec^d and the registered package is in P. O. according to notice rec$^{d.}$

I wrote fully to Buck the other day and asked him to confer with you, as I was too busy to write again.

You are I know with us heart and hand. We have, in

our Cause, a good and a reasonable thing. We should therefore carry it on properly. No autocrats can exist in it in office, although privately there may be autocratically disposed members.

With the private character of no man do I propose to concern myself unless it is vital for all. If C were a bad man I would not care so long as he carried on our T. S. business properly. But I am convinced he is *not* the man to be on our Board and I have so told him and shall try to get him off of it. I consider him on it as a detriment to all.

He intends to claim that the Board is a fixture and that no changes can be made on it. This is bosh. It is contrary to the genius of the T S. The T. S. has a regular council and elects officers annually. My plan is and I think you will second it, and I ask for suggestions, to have an *American Theosophical Council,* which annually elects a Pres^t, Secy and Executive Com., all subject to the Parent Society and Council. The Am. C^l to be elected by delegates from each Branch, or by proxy from the Branches. Drop then the name of *American Board of Control.* It is not a good name but leads to erroneous ideas. This C has assumed to be the autocrat and all because of that name. And he induced you and Buck to agree to that resolution in 1885 about his being the censor of the Am. P. R. Socy — more Rot — so that he might have more authority. We must have harmony, and we cannot as he proceeds.

I do not object to a N. Y. Branch No. 2, *as such,* but I do object to his going at it in that way. Why up to date the Aryan T. S. has not heard a word about any such new thing. This is irregular and not frank.

If some N Y people do not like publicity, let them plainly say so and ask for a private Branch and then keep to themselves. To that I do not object. I would let in cranks, Jesuits — anybody — for I know that if the leaders keep the objects plainly in front, the cranks and Jesuits will be *nil* because they can find no place for their plans. But if we have autocracy, secrecy and concealed knowledge only for selected souls then we go to pieces.

Theosophy is strong just because in India there is no secrecy and those only get secrets who compel them and who know how to keep them.

Read and return the enclosed, *via* Buck.

As Ever

WILLIAM Q JUDGE

May 28, 1886

My dear Mrs. Waters:

I have been thinking for some days of two serious things. Now that Arthur [Gebhard] is going away I am left so to say with no one to act near to me, and so perhaps my mind may be getting active.

The thing first of importance is the question, What do our members think of the Cause and how far are they willing to turn that into practice? I know that you are willing to and do as far as you can turn it into practice, for you teach your daughter the things you learn yourself, as far as she is able to take them. So also does Dr Buck, whose entire family of six are brought up in that way. This is a most important point, and I feel very strongly that it is one we should have impressed upon the minds of all. There are many persons studying with us who do not say one word to their children, but allow them to go on imbibing the false theories of the current religion, weakly hoping that when the children shall have grown up, the errors can be corrected. How unjust this is to the children who are thus filled up with obstacles to future progress. Surely, if members believe there is anything in Karma or Reincarnation, how easy to tell the children. They ought to hold weekly meetings for the benefit of the latter where they might be offered proper spiritual food. The good done in this way is not to be calculated. Of course I do not mean that you ought to rush out and establish schools, but I just tell you what I think so that you may tell others whom you know and then perhaps after a while many people will think in the same way.

It will tend to correct many errors which I see already springing up through the misdirected notions of theosophists who are leaning and longing after psychic culture. For I know that a good many persons are so hankering after what they call "knowledge and light" but which in reality is a desire to find occult power, that they are willing to hunt all through the Theosophical Society for it but are not willing to put the society publicly on its true philosophical and moral basis, nor do they say aught to their children. Many of them say "we will not belong to an organization," but we want to study occultism, and some theosophists are not willing to lose what seems possible material for the Cause. But the children of today are the adults of a few years hence, and if in some way they can be put on the right track, so much the better for the race of which they will themselves in turn be the guides.

Your words on this subject to the Boston Theosophists and to the liberal minded among your friends, have great weight and might cause large and wide spreading trees of deed and thought to grow up.

For myself I must wait. I would that I had naught to do but to continually go about among Theosophists and others spreading these doctrines. But I must wait in patience I suppose.

The next question is regarding many people in Boston who have not joined the Society for various reasons. Is there any possibility of their joining the N Y Branch while they are waiting the Coues developments? They could do this and remain unknown if such was their wish, and at any time withdraw for the purpose of forming a body of their own in Boston. I thought perhaps if I could solidify all theosophists and inquirers by these notes of ours — now small but easily enlarged — much good would be done. I shall write all the Branches to try and get a fund started for a general monthly Abridgment: all questions and replies and discussion notes to go to one place, say here and then to be printed after proper editing and distributed to all. I printed 300 last month and they are all gone now, such is the demand.

I suppose the task of editing say 8 pages per month

would be putting too much on your shoulders. But Baxter could do it. — We here are not striving to claim the honors, we only wish the work done. It seems well to do it here; but I must confess it is rapidly assuming larger proportions than I dreamed of — and am satisfied that very soon so many questions (replies are nil) will come along that 4 pages will not do.

There is a Los Angeles, Cal. member who proposes a genuine headquarters out there. What do you think of it. I told her to go ahead.

The Coues affair will be all right in July. He will not be pres^t after that. The result will be all right then I think.

Regarding vacation, I never take any. It is impossible for me to be one moment still. I have many invitations to all parts of the world and some I would like to accept. One was to Europe from H. P. B. It had to be shelved.

I do not know that it is possible for me to explain to you how I feel. An immense irresistible current drives me on, and continually I feel that I am wasting, losing or playing with valuable time. But of course I am not. Many people misconstrue me, and perhaps often I fear that I am unable to see into the darkness of my own self. The self is like a glove. You see it; you take it off, and yet there is the darkness of the inside, and inside there is the darkness and also the inside surface, all unknown.

I have sometimes gone away but when in the country I have felt lost, for no one cared to think or speak of the higher things, the immensely greater things there are than the foolish current that surges around us. Then again, you know I am married and I cannot go off to pleasant places leaving Mrs Judge behind. She is cultivated enough, but not a theosophist, and I fear has a prejudice against it hard to be overcome. Mrs Cushman invited me to Bar Harbor but it seems to me that I cannot go there.

Taking everything all round, I will say frankly to you in confidence, that very often I feel a great longing to escape from all this, from America, from Europe from all. The world has no charms for me and I have many things it seems in my character that *grind* upon people. It may be my intense convictions my intense beliefs and the sure confidence I have. Did I not have it I could not stay with these people, for with it I know that all is Karma and that Karma is divine, intelligent and just above all things. In Karma then I put my trust. One man accuses me of objects of ambition, another of tyranny, another of harshness. But I cannot please them all and so must go on in my way for "death in the performance of your own duty according to your own way is preferable," and I cannot do either the duty, or according to the dictates of the duty, of another. I suppose this year Mr. Olcott will give me a week's vacation — when I do not know and have no plan made for such an event. Last year I had a week at Christmas and spent it with Buck where a society of 25 now has sprung up.

I never wished Arthur to do anything on S——'s promise and advised against it. I think I know the reason for the curious acts you refer to. It may be something else besides insanity — perhaps a temporary result of something. She is sick and takes much medicine and perhaps it had a bad effect. Do not fear I will incur any expense on

31

any body's promise. I have seen too many broken, as is usual.

There is a sanscrit grammar by one Gunn or Ginn published in Boston. Will look at my copy tonight and send you the name and address on the card. Whitney's grammar is very advanced and seems difficult.

Hoping to have the advantage of a conversation with you in the near future — perhaps the wheel of fate will make a sudden, wild erratic turn — I beg to remain

Fraternally yours

WILLIAM Q. JUDGE.

Regards to Mr. Waters, Hope and Miss Guernsey.

Louise A Off   June 3 1886

Dear Madam

Your letter of May 14 came to me like a breath of that pure atmosphere you describe, and the project it contains is one with which I feel personally very much in sympathy.

One unfortunate thing in American Theosophy is the want of leisure for self culture on the part of theosophists. Most of us have our daily routine of business and the complicated "Wants" of our civilization compel by far the larger number of our members to live externally as the world does. The institution you speak of would necessarily be for those who are so far independent in means and in other circumstances as to have leisure, and for them I think there can be no question about its great advantages. You may remember that Light on the Path speaks of periods of growth and silence, followed by periods of action, and I think that it is just as true that people feel compelled in time to go forth to teach what they have learned as that they feel impelled to seek seclusion in order to learn and to develop in themselves the things they afterwards impart to others. Now, if this be true, such an institution as you speak of would be eminently useful to those who are willing to give their lives to the cause of Theosophy. It would be a home for those who gave up every other home, and a centre from which Theosophy all over America might gather strength and gain light.

Such a place as you desire to make would, in fact, beyond question be a spiritual centre. At Adyar in India, we have the headquarters, and no doubt it forms a centre, not only from which forces radiate, but also towards which aspirations tend and it does much towards solidifying the whole body of Theosophists. Any member can go there, and stay a short time, but it is not in any sense a Lamasery. All who are there are present for work, and not for any kind of play. It is the centre of the ever busy work of the society. Inasmuch as we are an Universal Brotherhood which thinks it has hold of some true doctrines, it is our duty to give out those rules of thought and conduct which the world so much needs; and this brings us to a question which arises concerning your proposal: Is it Buddhistic, or Hindu, or Esoterically Christian, or what? And the mere statement of the question seems to point at once to one conclusion — that the place ought to be started as a purely theosophic retreat or head-quarters, thus permitting any-one who is a member to feel at home although he may belong to some particular religious body.

This very important desideratum for the institution, namely Universality or "catholicity," does not seem com-patible with making it in any special sense a lamasery, for the element which binds the members of a lamasery is the possession of a particular and limited creed. If you intend that Theosophy in general should be the cementing force there are two difficulties that suggest themselves at once. The first is the difficulty that would be experienced in mak-ing a secluded retreat, such as would be necessary for the spiritual development you speak of, compatible with an active centre of work and propaganda, which latter is not only a most important point at present for theosophy, but, as I said before, those who secluded themselves, would after a while be obliged by their own feelings to go into this active work of propaganda. It is found in practice that the large majority of men do not get out of these alter-nating periods of seclusion and activity for a long time, perhaps during several incarnations, for to be able to leave the world for ever presupposes a very high degree of spirit-ual development, for it means that that person's sphere of usefulness and activity has become one which is higher than the physical plane of existence.

The second difficulty consists in this, that anyone who had advanced so far as to be capable of such a life as that implied by the idea of a Theosophical lamasery would naturally gravitate to India, where the heads of the Society live, I mean the Brothers of the First section. You must remember that we are all brothers of the third section (the lowest) in this country. When any theosophist has advanced into the second section he becomes a chela and comes under the personal guidance and teaching of some brother of the first section, and at a certain point in his development it becomes necessary for him to live in proximity with his Master. It seems to me that to give the institution at all the true character of a Theosophic lamasery all three sections of the society should be represented in it, so that, as matters now stand, it could at best be no more than a preparatory school, as it were, from which the aspirants for a degree must pass to a higher college or university.

You are probably as well aware as I am that ages of experience have proved that the greatest progress is not made by those who retire from the sight of men. Those who have progressed and are now retired made their progress first, before their retirement, and passed away because that very progress, which was obtained among men made it impossible for them to remain in the scenes and under the influences which they had passed beyond. So then, all singleminded theosophists here ought to know that the thing which will make their progress rapid is unselfish work in trying to lift their fellow men up to a higher plane.

Now the west has no real central Theosophic point as yet. Perhaps Los Angeles may become it. It is a beautiful situation — I was there once and know it.

If you had a real headquarters there, which was devoted to the work I have indicated, work which is in fact the most conducive to the progress of the individual as well as that of the Society, and where no foolish worldly talk or vain formalities prevailed, then it would soon be known as a place devoted to the cause where inquirers would be helped to understand the movement, and thus to understand themselves.

In Rochester Mrs. J. W Cables has a somewhat similar place to that I describe. She has a home there where she permits theosophists to stay, and she explains to them as much as she can. Many persons have become theosophists owing to her; and she has a little paper devoted to the cause. She is a vegetarian.

So it seems to me that a beginning ought to be made in that modest way. If you call it a Lamasery it will excite ridicule and create erroneous impressions. Let those who are going to take charge of the matter select their house or build it. Let them own it either in common, or in whatever way they decide; then devote it to the uses of the Los Angeles branch, remove all personalities from its atmosphere; let it be known that it is not a wonder seeking, or astral hunting place, but a centre for true philanthropic and brotherly thought and feeling. Of course all rules for its government, and for visitors – how they should be admitted, how long they should stay etc – will grow out of your own good judgment.

The Masters have said in writing and everybody will soon be convinced that the Society and its work must prosper on its moral and philosophical strength and not by phenomena. This is also true of the units of which it is composed, and the greatest progress for and benefit from the movement will be due to those devoted men and women who while they keep together and give life to just such an institution as you propose, at the same time work hard and unselfishly to bring others to a knowledge of the true doctrine.

I know well that there is a great field for the cause in the west, and it sadly needs some centre of energy to which all enquirers can be referred. Let us hope that Los Angeles will furnish that centre.

Such a place can do a great deal. It would have all the literature of Theosophy, and its correspondence would show just what the needs and feelings of enquirers were, thus enabling us to know just what ought to be done from time to time. In fact there is a big future before such an institution.

However I must await further letters from you as I have no idea of what the plans really and in detail are. But if in using the word "Lamasery" you mean exactly what that implies in Tibet then I cannot agree as to its advisability yet. I do however think that what I have been talking of is a good thing, and if those who start it and manage it, are in reality themselves "living the life" then their influence will be all the greater, and they will beyond question attract to them certain Hindu disciples of the Masters who know more than we do as yet, and who are not so very far away.

Believe me, dear Madam,
yours fraternally
WILLIAM Q. JUDGE

Dear Buck   July 13 1886

Your long, good, letter at hand and you will see I anticipated it in my last letter. Why is it you and I have not quarreled at all although we disagree? I suppose because we are both gentlemen as well as students of occultism. I have never worked under the board although broken reeds have been my support.

Let me have Hermetic article soon. Awfully obliged to you as I am overworked indeed.

Blow all the winds smack the cheek I silent am if all the same I break.

Yes, the copy sent by request. Love to all. As ever

WILLIAM Q.

I only fight for ideas and foundations and such are those Adyar C[l] has adopted, to be adhered to at risk of disintegration.

————

I. B. Rumford, Esq   New York, Aug 3 1886
Dear Sir and Bro:

I thank you for the subscription of the Golden Gate Lodge to *The Path*. All the numbers have been sent and I hope are safe to hand.

I do not think that the fundamental ideas of what is known as mind cure, are admitted by many, if any, theosophists in the sense they are apparently understood by the expounders of that System, and mind cure science is as yet in its infancy. There is probably much still to be found out about it. I am not aware that Madame Blavatsky ever

38

claimed any such power over her own health, as that you assert she *ought* to have according to the mind cure theories, while at the same time I *believe* she possesses it, and knows the fact that she does so.

If it be true that the advocates of mind cure have discovered *a* means of curing disease which was unknown before that system was invented, the discovery will be a most valuable one for suffering humanity, and I have no doubt it will be a welcome addition to practical occultism, but it does not seem to be *Theosophy,* nor an adequate equivalent for it, nor do I see why we should call Mind Cure "Western Theosophy."

The peculiar and truly magical power which you use to cure disease has long been known in mesmerism under the name of "the power of suggestion," or of the "fixed idea," and it is vaguely recognized by medical science by the very inappropriate name of "imagination." The limits to which this power will go in the case of some individuals has not yet been fixed, but I would draw your attention to this fact, that this power, with which initiates of occult science are very familiar, is one of those which are known to be most dangerous to meddle much with *unless you are an initiate.* It is a power as easily used for evil as for good, and those who are strongly endowed with it find themselves open to new and strong temptations when they discover that they possess it. In the case of those whose moral nature is proof against this temptation to abuse the power, there is still another danger, for its effects are so wonderful that they believe themselves possessed of far more knowledge and power than they really have, *and this is liable to cause a complete arrest of Spiritual development,* unless the proper place of the powers in the system of universal Science known as Theosophy be perceived and acknowledged.

You may perhaps ask why Madame Blavatsky does not cure herself if, as I believe, she has that power, and knows that she possesses it. You must remember that curing bodily disease, and restoring physical health is not the "be all and end all." Philosophy as well as religion has always taught that the soul is purified and strengthened by suffering, and it is sometimes well to suffer. If we could know the action and operation of Karma we would see that by suffering pain in sickness bad Karma is worked off which could not be got rid of if one be suddenly cured as in "mind cure." Those who know and recognize this fact are cured thereby of the mental distress which is so large a part of the evil of bodily suffering, and this is for them a "mind cure" on a higher plane than the physical, for then they can bear their sufferings with calmness and resignation.

But I do not disparage your action, I only wish you not to misunderstand Madame Blavatsky or other theosophists who may, for all that you can know, choose to suffer from ill health. It is certain that the desire to heal others springs from unselfishness, and in so far it is good. Remember, however, the words of Jesus when he healed: "Be whole, *thy sins are forgiven*" which interpreted by Theosophy means: "Thy bad Karma is worked off; there is no more need that thou shouldst suffer."

May you all prosper and come to realize the true.

yours fraternally
WILLIAM Q JUDGE.

40

A. P. Sinnett Esq   New York Aug 9/86
My dear sir.

I am in receipt of your article entitled "Theosophic Morals," and, as H. P. B. in the letter she sent in the same envelope directs, it will appear in September Path without any alteration. I need not say that I am very glad to have an article of yours for the Magazine, because you must be aware of the fact, and if more contributions were received from different individuals the Path perhaps would not savor so strongly of one mind. I have done my best to conceal identity, for I know general readers do not like to eternally listen to one man, but I fear after a while they will pierce through the thin veil of words. I had however hoped that your first contribution would be upon some other theme where personalities would not enter. At this distance and in this country people do not look at the matter in controversy just as it is regarded by the small circle of European Theosophists, who may be said to live in a continual blaze, limited to a small area. The American branches are scattered over immense spaces and Mohini and Babajee are really unknown. No one here, with say two exceptions know who Murdhna Joti is, and therefore every reader has looked at the article as the expression of individual opinion only. The policy of the Path always will be to give all sides of these questions and it must not be supposed that the people at large look at the terminology used from any than their own standpoint, and not from the higher mystical one which latter is yours and that of the European theosophists. A grave error of position is being constantly committed, if you will allow me to say so, by theosophists always assum-

41

ing the attitude of chelas and construing all utterances from that point of view, whereas that attitude should be always reserved for private conversation — if allowed at all.

If my opinion were asked on the Higher Life paper, I would not agree with all of it, but am certainly of opinion that certain great souls now and then do incarnate to carry on great reforms or works while other great ones carry on in another sphere — without incarnation — the same work. And I do not see that Masters are impugned thereby. The perfect household life *must* then be illustrated by somebody as *all* cannot be great, or little, chelas. And this idea is contained in the article as I look at it.

Give my regards to Mrs Sinnett, and believe me to be
very truly yours
W. Q. JUDGE

P. S. I should say that this is written without reading your paper, as I do not intend to read it until it is in proof.

Dear Buck:
Aug 23, 1886

"Come Antony and young Octavius come; revenge yourselves alone on Cassius; for Cassius is aweary of the world. Hated by one he loves scorned by his brother: All his faults observed."

Arthur is pitching into me for *not* going to C and you — you — you

Your letter has good advice which I accept, but it is full of baseless things. . . .

All your remarks about what "others" — unnamed — tell

42

you I ignore until I have their names. As yet they exist not for me.

Twice before I almost resolved only to write you on philosophy and *not* any more to confide in you my feelings not given to other men. This letter is my reward. Now I resolve. All business letters shall be official, and while I retain my love for you and shall call on you for help in the cause, I shall not attempt to take you into my deep confidence as you always seem to suppose I am in the same way talking to others.

Your head is *not* cut off, as the orders state that the Council is to be composed of Pres^t and *also* of the present B of C. So resign if you please. Yes, take a good heart and head of the Board and leave it to C and P. Two fine fellows. They will be pleased; I will be sorry.

Very plainly I wrote you that all I thought was that the Convention should meet and that I didnt care who was elected. It would probably be C as I nor you would scheme to get it nor make political moves. Furthermore he will always keep the thing prominent. My God, could I plainer write. And yet you lower me to the plane expressed in your letter. . . .

I do not wish, nor shall I be dragged into fights. . . . So let us drop it all. Let you and me rise into the light alone of philosophy and as to work and business in the Society we dont exist together.

My Branch persisted in passing a resolution of inquiry. I do not want to do aught but wait. But on me will fall the odium of it.

I made an error about the arteries. So consider I said

valves in the veins. Going through the lung is purification by fire, through moisture, etc etc. But the other facts I want.
                                        Love to all
                                    Your loving brother
                                            WILLIAM Q

S. Govina Row Sattay Esq   Aug. 25, 1886
My dear Sir and brother
    Your letter to Bro. Joshi has been handed me, in which you request his aid in getting you out of jail. While I sympathize with you, and shall try to aid you in this matter, and can see that the Association acted contrary to their supposed religion, I cannot endorse the wisdom of your proceeding which caused you trouble. No one is more opposed to Christianity than I am, but I fail to see by what right you invaded the premises of these people and gathered listeners round you without leave. That is not freedom; it is license. No missionary in India would be allowed to enter a sacred temple and propagate his religion or run down the other. He would be arrested by the authorities. This camp where you were, is for them devoted to their absurd religion, and you had no right to go there except quietly. Had you held your meeting outside in the road, they could have done nothing.
    Therefore you do right in asking their pardon no matter how wrong they are. I hope they will let you out. Legally

I do not see any other way for the offense was no doubt committed.

I am also sorry to see that you write Joshee that there is no freedom here unless one pretends to christianity. Such a course is wrong and very unnecessary. The Vedas say that you must not revile the gods of other men. Karma often follows quickly on such an act. I like you violently oppose Christianity which is really very weak here, but I would be mad to rush into their places of worship and preach contrary-wise. But you tried in the one place where they are strong.

I should be sorry to see you pretend to Christianity. If you do you will be reviled by these people; if you do not, you will have the respect and aid of the hosts of non Christian people who are all over this land.

Joshee spoke against the religion in Boston and was well received but it was in a hall where free speech prevails.

I will go down to Asbury Park today and try to see Stokes and do what I can for you. I do not know where your things are but will try and find them.

Hoping you will be soon released,

I am fraternally yours

WILLIAM Q JUDGE

F. T. S.

P. O. Box 2659 N. Y.

S. Govina Row Sattay   Aug. 31 1886

Dear Sir and Brother:

My name, which you could not read, is, Wm Q. Judge. I am pres^t of the N Y Theosophical Society and one of the founders of the Society whose headquarters now are in India, at Madras, and I was there in 1884.

I saw the N Y Sun about your case and they put in an account, and now a Herald reporter wants to see you about it.

I did not mean that you had disturbed their services or blasphemed but that you had committed sufficient offence for them as they own the *whole* of Ocean Grove and can exclude any one they like. I thought you were injudicious for I know the temper of these bigots. Next time you will not be caught. In any public place you can say what you please but not in a place like that.

You have sympathizers everywhere.

I went down to Ocean Grove and found you had got out and gone away and was sorry I missed you. So I did the next best thing which was to fully ventilate your case in the N Y Sun and it has now gone over the whole country. I will show your letter to the Herald man and perhaps he may put in some more which will give those people at Ocean Grove a good public flogging which they deserve.

Sincerely yours
WILLIAM Q. JUDGE.

Mrs. Helen L. Sumner: Sept. 25 1886

Madame:

In reply to yours of 23d instant in which you ask about joining the Aryan Theosophical Society of New York, I beg to say:

We have no desire to cause members to withdraw from other Branches, but rather wish to see all solidified in interest all over the country. It was for that reason that the A. T. S. started the *Abridgments of Discussions,* so as to afford to distant members the chance to communicate their thoughts, and also that they might feel united with other minds than their own. That is the only way we could hit on for meeting the needs of those who cannot attend meetings, and that is all non resident members would get in return for membership — excepting of course the unseen but strong help which arises from unconscious communion of mind. . . .

In answer to your question about the Path, I would say, that our intention is to carry it on. I do not remember stating anywhere that its continuance depends on the help accorded in the first year. . . .

It is very pleasant to have your praise of The Path. Its motive is solely to try and offer here some good doctrines and help to earnest souls.

The H. B. of L. did some good to earnest people but I long ago knew — although I never joined it — that the Hindu [Hermetic] Brotherhood of Luxor would not last.

If all theosophists will try to separate chaff from wheat, and rest on the idea that there is no separateness one from the other, and at the same time *try* for themselves

47

and unceasingly *try* to aid on the spiritual progress of others, our cause cannot fail. Masters have *written* that we will prosper on moral and philosophical worth but never by phenomena.

Fraternally yours

WILLIAM Q. JUDGE

Dear Sexton: —   Oct 8, 1886
    Yours of 4th at hand.

Too rapidly you have concluded that no one read the true inner nature of the person you allude to, because — without knowing what others thought — I had a very clear view of the said mediumistic condition. But the line between medium and non medium is very shadowy. Many persons who think they are not mediums are really so. All mediums are not bad. Many who suppose they are mediums are in fact not mediums. If I could be the medium of the progressed entities of Satwa-Yuga, I would willingly accept. Do not let us assume to judge any one absolutely. Mediums are sensitives upon a material plane.

As to the Secret Section, it does not depend wholly upon you or me who shall be admitted. It probably has grades in it. Its work is, not to give evidences or "certificates" to its members, but to aid by personal influence our fellow men and thus to spread real theosophical doctrine and life. So, it must follow, that personal ambitions and any sort of narrowness are not found within it. This being

48

so, one would find some working in it by methods not ours; but no judgment should be passed thereupon.

There might be many working in this Section and yet we never actually know it, however much we might surmise. The real point is, that those who work in it try to have the right motives, no matter what their methods are, due to education and personal idiosyncrasy. For instance, you might *know* that I was in it with yourself, and I might know of others (and you too) but never tell each other unless by request. Or in other words, we must respect and hold inviolate each other's desire not to refer to the existence of our membership in the section by *words,* no matter how convincing the proof which in *our actions* would appear that we are in the section. I know one person who, if asked, might deny adherence to theosophical organizations but who really does a great deal for the cause of theosophy. All this is not Jesuitry but reality. For nature, working toward reunion with the great All, manifests many varieties often at war with each other, yet all members of the great whole.

Very truly yours

WILLIAM Q. JUDGE.

————

My dear Page:

I have yours containing call for convention of T. S. at Cincinnati on Oct 30th.

Your telegram was not answered as I had no answer. A little delay, after so much on your side does not count much.

As to what you call "gross perversion of language," I see that the words in the order are "as soon as may be convenient." The notice in Path was from a copy of the order made by another person who probably read it wrong. I never looked at the Path again about that. Anyway, under the circumstances "as soon as possible" is not different from "as convenient." Such is my opinion.

Then "gross perversion" thus used by you unqualifiedly means "wilful perversion." It might have been well for you to have asked me if it *was* "wilful." Then again the Path is not official and therefore what it says can be of no consequence to you or any one else who wishes to construe official orders.

I dont know what "feeling in parts of the U. S." you refer to. I know all about the feeling and just where it is located, and know that the aggregate of feeling is that time has been wasted and that the Society and the Cause has been brought into great disrepute, and that autocracy has been made the watchword of the movement. That must come to an end. It is ended.

I do not mean you: you know who I mean. And I have letters enough over signature to open your eyes if they are not open now.

Why cant we push on this movement unselfishly, and not squabble over "recognition or help" or place or position.

If you have a grievance against me, as you have often said to others, why dont you give it straight to me and not to others. By all right I am the one to hear of it first and not by indirection.

As far as I know there are only 11 U. S. Branches and they are weak. The 2^d N Y Branch had never met when July meeting was held nor has the Phil one yet. Besides the 2^d N Y one and its organizers say they do not like the "common people" who are in the T. S. This may be a new kind of theosophy. But as the 2^d N Y are under the impression that they hear weekly or monthly from an Adept of high degree who temporarily for the purpose occupies the senses of one present, they may feel justified in their sentiments. It is not for me to judge them.

I shall submit your printed notice to the A. T. S. at an early meeting.
Fraternally
WILLIAM Q JUDGE

Nov. 4 1886

Dear Aldrich

Bro Harte returned from Cincinnati — with his statement of what occurred but as I have no minutes nor copy nor have heard from Page, I do not know officially.

I had hoped to go, but at the last moment Mr. Olcott rushed off to Cuba and I had to remain. That is the sole reason why we sent Harte, for no other member had the spare time.

From his account I should suppose that a misunderstanding arose at first which happily was quieted as he says by your judicious intervention. Buck also misunderstood me, for he said to me he thought I had sent Harte for some reason other than above, whereas in fact the Branch sent him and for no other reason.

It appears the convention met and constituted itself, and thought it wise not to pass any other rules. Perhaps that will turn out to be just as well, except that it might have been more definite to have set a day for reassembling. I suggested to Harte that he propose for your consideration that in future representation in council should be by elected delegates and not by Pres^{ts} as a pres^{t} might be not harmonious with the Branch, but that of course went over with the rest.

Today I have a letter from the California Branches expressing pleasure that there is now a Council as they say they felt neglected by never hearing from anybody and having neither Charters nor certificates of membership. This of course is small, but people have to be pleased I suppose with these things.

Buck wrote me some while ago that you might go to India, and I replied saying that all the Branches east would make you delegate for them. Did he tell you? Please let me know when (if) you are going so that I may get you the papers making you their delegate at the next convention.

By the way, talking of supposed neglect, do you know that up to this hour I have no information about the Indian convention. A notice was sent here, and I suppose was received by somebody but none of us have heard of it. Of those matters H. S. Olcott does not write me as he supposes I am duly at once informed here. Will you oblige me by some information on the point as I suppose you and Buck have seen or heard of the thing.

Referring again to the convention of Oct 29, I will say that I felt sure in advance that it would go on right no matter what was done, for I had some reliable information in advance which may be symbolized in this way:

A large strong steamship running aground in an icy bay. It stops. The captain and officers got off and went away up a road into the icy country. Meanwhile ship bound in the ice but unhurt. All the people did not go off of her.

One passenger went ashore to reconnoitre and met there a man who had some connection with the ship. They returned together and suddenly the ice parted, they started up the machinery and the ship steamed bravely out slowly at first and taking bearings and advice from old sailor at the point, and reached at last a goal.

The icy bay was Cincinnati and the ice was the coagulation which at first appeared but was dissipated by you. I do not yet quite know the dark man who returned on board with the passenger. I suspect you.

But whatever or whoever, I am as sure of the propriety of what was done and of the final success as I am of this sheet of paper, no matter who may leave the ship or how they go. I pity those who went for that land was horribly cold, bare and desolate.

As ever sincerely yours,
WILLIAM Q JUDGE.

A. W. Barnard Esq   Nov 16, 1886

Dear Sir

I think you are about right in not expecting to "obtain much mystic power" from our Society. We do not profess to supply it. We are a body of earnest students, and try to the best of our power to live up to our professions, in which I fear many of us fail. Those professions are founded upon the morality which is common to every age and every religion (at least as far as lip service goes). But we make no external professions, and live as unobtrusively as we can, making our professions only in our own hearts, and wearing the "yellow robe" internally.

The fact is that many people in these times apply the commercial spirit to things spiritual. "I am ready to pay for powers, and for knowledge of the occult; you have the supply, then favor me with some of your wares." Of course I do not mean that anyone offers money, but they offer promises of a life's devotion etc.

Now, My dear sir, the old rule still remains in force in things occult: that knowledge is only given to those who deserve it, and have proved by their life that they do deserve it. Only those who do the will of the Masters are reckoned as deserving their notice; aspirations, desires, promises go for nothing. What is that will? Well, it is simply to free your mind from vain and earthly desires, and to work at the work before you always lending a helping hand to others. Get rid of anger, of vanity, pride, resentfulness, ambition and *really lose them,* and you have then made the first step towards the understanding of the occult; with these feelings latent in the heart it is not possible to make one single step in magic.

54

You may acquire psychic power, and no doubt there are men in India and elsewhere who can help you in that direction, but it would be to your destruction eventually. They are the quacks of Occultism — beware of them. Their plane of work is the psychic, not the spiritual — the region of delusions, not that of truth.

As a society The Theosophical Society is exoteric. Its work is above board and open — namely to encourage its members in studying the ancient Doctrine and in "leading the life." The esoteric work does not appear, and cannot appear, because it is between the individual member and a source which reaches him only through his own inner consciousness.

Hence our Society is disappointing to those who expect to learn how to draw magic figures and pronounce magic words which will "raise the devil" or make water turn into wine. But for him who can see below the surface of things it is the first step in a brotherhood at whose head stand the adepts of the Himalayas.

Many men approach the subject of occultism in the way you seem to have done — with a wish to produce effects. They find that the only terms on which they will be taught (not by their fellow students) is to "lead the life," and that to have made the leading of the life habitual is the only preparation for the acquirement of occult powers, and by the time those powers come they are looking to something higher and they seem to them trivial, childish, only useful for making the ignorant stare or envy them — for "showing off" as children say. Yours very truly

W. Q. Judge (by R. H.)

55

N. Y., Mar 21 1887

My dear Dr. Coues:

. . . . Referring to H P B. you will well understand my position when I tell you that as far back as 1874 she (and others) outlined to me this whole movement as it has gone on since, and I am very well satisfied, by many proofs, that the Karma of the T S. and of all Western members is indissolubly bound up with hers.

They little dream of the significance of this and go on heaping up more and more instead of lightening the load she has to bear.

I am very truly yours

WILLIAM Q JUDGE

F. A. Nims Esq   April 5, 1887
Dear Sir

By the suggestion of Col J C Bundy I write you. You will I hope excuse my writing upon paper belonging to another matter than that which is the subject of this; but the fact is that the general secys office of the T. S. here is slim in funds and all its work is done gratuitously by several persons.

The policy of the real movers of the Theosophical Society is (when people really listen and believe) to help all sincere students, and also to try to help theosophists. To that end Branches or groups are encouraged to be formed not as being exclusive, nor yet as being universal.

There are some members in Muskegon talking of a Branch, but if you desire to join the T. S. and to have your own group there can be no objection to it. Every group ought to work sincerely for the common good, and yet each is entitled to its own freedom and autonomy, and to manage its affairs, within theosophical lines, just as it sees fit.

What method do you wish to pursue? Are you and your friends desirous of pursuing occultism as such, or of studying philosophically, or as enthusiastic adherents of a cause whose aim is to raise as far as possible the race — to put it esoterically: "of lifting some of the heavy Karma of the world"? You need not if you are so minded reply to that query. In regard to tyros "going in" for occultism strictly, there are two things to ponder over — very old: "All hope is given up by those who enter here," and, "it is easy perhaps to rush into the centre of the conclave but what is the method of escaping?"

As to the latter I can only say with my present lights, that while one may enter the "circle of ascetics" forcibly and vehemently, no retrogression can be made except by an acquaintance with the orderly and *fixed* method. All of the foregoing relates to the query regarding occultism strictly so called and is not at all meant as discouragement. . . .

After hearing from you I can write further.

Believe me to be sir

Yours sincerely

WILLIAM Q JUDGE

Gen¹ Secʸ T. S., U. S.

35 Broadway
N. Y. July 20 1887.

Mrs. M. L. Brainard,
Dear Madame:

I have yours of 11th in regard to Dr. Phelon in which you give your private views and ask inquiries for private use; and I beg to say that this reply is also to be considered as expressing my personal opinions only and not in any sense as official.

In the first place let me say that I did not delegate Col. Ayme for the purpose referred to by you nor for any purpose. As he was in Chicago and disinterested, I asked him as a personal favor to let me know about the proposal regarding a new Branch of which I had heard. Any other proceedings he may have taken rest entirely with himself.

As a general reply to your letter I might justly say (and put it also as a question) that none of us can claim a monopoly of theosophy nor of Branch work.

You say that "most of your members belong outside of" Chicago. This would in itself show perhaps that it is not strictly doing Chicago work. But in my opinion the fact does not militate against the Branch.

§ 6 of Art. III of the Cons^t· expressly states that the number of Branches in any town is unlimited. § 8 says 5 or more persons may get a Charter. § 14 continues the T. S. general rules in force. In those you will find that express provision is made that people who desire to form a Branch having distinct leanings in whatever directions, composed of coreligionists or those of a similar cult, may form it and shall be allowed to do so. If you and I do not

58

agree with Spiritualists or Catholics, we have no right to say that they shall not have a charter provided they subscribe to the 3 objects of the Society, or only to the first.

This is the very object we have in view, i.e.: to have as many differently constituted Branches as possible so that we may get into the sphere and influence of theosophy as many beings as possible. What right then have we to say to people that they cannot come in and cannot form Branches unless they believe just as we do, viz: in opposition to spiritualism? There is no such right.

For my part I have long regretted the fact that we had no spiritualist Branch. That is just what is wanted. For if we had some such, we might reach many who are now just ripe for Theosophy, and need only the explanations which Theosophy offers. The facts of spiritualism are there and cannot be evaded. But how are we to draw the lessons and explain the facts if we have no strength of membership in any of our Branches? The Spiritualists are now to my personal knowledge ready for our *philosophy* and we here in the west ought to use their *facts*. For 40 years they have experimented and agree that they have had no philosophy and need it. It seems that if a chance arises to interject the beneficial influences of Theosophy, it would be followed by good results.

As to Dr. Phelon, I can constitute myself no man's judge. I should never try to force my opinions into his mind, nor extract any other pledge from him than that which he has already given, viz: to support universal brotherhood and *toleration*. I am not greater than Masters, and they have long abided my ignorance and folly as well as the errors of many good supporters of their efforts. How then shall I judge Dr. Phelon or anybody else in small matters.

As to "shells" being Presidents of Branches, I cannot offer now any pertinent opinion inasmuch as the question has not arisen in practice. When it does it then will be the time to act on that.

There is a sentence in your letter I will quote. You say, referring to Brother Sexton — whom I have known a long time and highly respect — "I certainly hope he will not be compelled to use unpleasant decisive measures, through outside manipulation regarding an extra Branch which is not needed just now, as most of our members belong outside of the City," and would say — without laying upon any person the full force of the quotation, — that "unpleasant decisive outside manipulation" is not strictly in the line of Theosophy. Such management as that certainly does not meet with your own calm approval. If any one should apply for another Charter for Chicago the matter would be referred to the Executive Committee and that Com^t would, and shall, notify Mr. Sexton or whoever was in charge of the Chicago T. S. If any objections were made they would be heard before any decision pro or con was reached. In this matter of Charters and theosophical work "manipulation" ought to be farthest from all our actions. The only "manipulation" that we ought to indulge in is that sort which, acting upon ourselves, causes us to sink any and all personal considerations for the good of the general work.

Now I have written at great length and hope the subject has been covered. Please read my letter in the same calm spirit in which I write it, as I have no personal interest whatever in any of these matters.

Sincerely and fraternally yours

WILLIAM Q JUDGE

J. V. Dales Esq   Dec 19, 1887

Dear Sir

I have your letter, and am glad to reply to any one sent by Mme Blavatsky. But I am sorry I cannot meet your wishes. I know of no society that answers your description, although I may not rightly understand you. The Shakers certainly do not. They are a religio-spiritualistic community, with peculiar views on sexual relations. My own experience in Occultism and in trying to live the Higher Life has conclusively shown me that we are placed by Karma wherever we may be and that we cannot gain by trying to "alter mere surroundings," we thus only run away from the very test given us for the object in view.

Any man can make a   *   in his own heart and there retire. But if he insists on finding such communities, my opinion is that they do not exist, as organizations, outside of India. In the U. S. they are unknown. The T. S. is the only society really pursuing occultism here, and many of its advanced students have reached the conclusions outlined above. Command me further.

I am sincerely yours

WILLIAM Q. JUDGE

* indecipherable

61

1888

Prof. Chas. H. Sykes   Jan. 31st, 1888
    San Francisco, Calif.
My dear Sir and Bro:

    . . . . It is lamentably true of Theosophical, as of all
other, Societies that the regular payment of regular dues
is a thing usually forgotten or disliked. Probably members do not realize that the expenses of an office are inces-
sant, and that those who contribute their time and labor as
an offering to the cause ought not to have the additional
care of a constant anxiety as to the receipts necessary for
the work. Generally speaking, it is no doubt true, as you
say, that "rules should be enforced." And yet one shrinks
from insisting on suspension or expulsion — the only available penalties — if dues are unpaid, especially when one
remembers that real poverty is sometimes the reason; and
all the more so when this would appear (however unjustly)
to give a certain mercenary tone to a Society of Brothers.
You can easily see the difficulties if you will think over the
whole topic in your own mind.

    My own conviction is, and has been, that, while every
member of the T. S. should feel it both his duty and his
privilege to sustain the Society by at least the prompt payment of his dues, it would be undesirable, perhaps disas-
trous, to attempt their collection by disciplinary measures,
and that all that can well be done is to set forth the great
need the office has for these small dues, and to suggest to
members that, whatever may be the indifference or the
shortcomings of others, each one may fulfil his own obligations and exhibit his own interest. I think, if you will ex-

pand this idea in your interviews with the Brethren near you, that they will see its justice and propriety.

Very truly and fraternally yours,

WILLIAM Q. JUDGE

Gen Sec'y T. S.

———

Mr. Wm. R. Savage,   Feb. 1st 1888

Baltimore, Md.

My dear Sir,

The questions you put refer rather to physical than to psychical matters. It is, of course, possible that mirages may be produced by nature-spirits, but the question is wholly speculative and of little practical moment. Ordinary scientific explanations seem adequate to account for them, and, when this is the case, I doubt the wisdom of seeking others more remote. Similarly as to the remarkable pink sunsets we so well remember, — so far, at least, as these have been explained.

I am so burdened with work and duties, personal, editorial, and official, that I have to ask your indulgence for a reply so brief.

Very truly and fraternally,

WILLIAM Q. JUDGE

The only available books on those sunsets are eastern ones in Sanscrit untranslated yet into English. Mirages have nothing to do with spiritual development. They occur also in cities in the East. Elementals are concerned in *all* the operations of nature.   J

66

My dear Harte,

The "Address to the Archbishop of Canterbury" is peculiarly able, well-conceived, and temperate, and two persons here expressed a wish that it should be printed and circulated as a pamphlet. . . .

I am very glad you like the "Epitome." Nearly 4000 have now been used. The plates have been electrotyped for permanent use. What did Madame say of it?

Where did Redway get his authority for raising the price of the Path? Am I to respond by exacting 14 shillings for "Lucifer"? Don't do anything about this. I'll attend to it.

I fear that Mrs. C.-O. does not sufficiently guard her tongue. We all, however, know Olcott too well to suspect him of littleness.

Ever yours,

WILLIAM Q JUDGE

Let your head fall off! No difficulty occurred about *the Densmores and they never applied to join the T. S.* and so I cant see why you didnt join application with H. P. B. In such company you ought to be willing to endorse the devil himself. How can we judge anybody, and is our T. S. such a holy body that only proved saints are permitted to enter it? If you don't like to put your name on the app[l] then sign mine to it.

In big hurry and will reply more fully soon.

Mr. J. F. Crawford,
Saratoga, Wyoming Territory.

My dear Sir and Bro,

I duly received your application and the accompanying $3.50, secured the counter-signatures of 2 members of the T. S., and have great pleasure in admitting and enrolling you as a *Member-at-Large.* I enclose your Diploma.

Your description of the conflicts and discouragements you undergo on the Way is a vivid and truthful picture of the experience *every one* encounters if making an honest and persistent effort to subdue the lower to the Higher Self. Now observe 2 things: 1st that the very strength of this lower self, thus asserting itself in vigorous resistance and in revival after defeat, is the best evidence of the need for the struggle, for, evidently, the greater the dominance of carnal impulses, the greater the reason for their overthrow; 2d that your regret over any failure in the fight proves on which side are your truest and deepest sympathies, and is thus an earnest of the time when there shall be no more failure and no more regret. If you did not care whether you lost or won, there would be ground for alarm; there is none so long as a defeat is followed by regret and *by a renewed effort.*

You will always find victory over evil thoughts most practicable if they are grappled with on first appearance and before making headway. It is for their reception and not for their appearance that one is responsible. A minister, once consulted on this topic, replied with an apt illustration: — "I cannot prevent the birds from flying over my

head, but I *can* prevent their making nests in my hair."
There is very much in this.

Do not expect to "drift" into calmer seas. You must "row" there. Progress comes from effort, not from inaction. And of the success of that effort there can be no question in any mind realizing the enormous advantage good has over evil.

I send you my best wishes and hopes, and am
Always truly and fraternally yours,

WILLIAM Q. JUDGE
Gen Sec T. S.

J. Ransom Bridge, Esq,   New York, Feb. 18, 1888
Pres^t Boston T. S.

Dear Sir and Bro: —

Your letter to the Aryan T. S. was submitted to that Society, who authorize me to reply to it, which I have pleasure in doing.

Your question is: "How does your Branch regard the 3^d of the Society's declared objects."*

After preliminary consideration the Branch first concluded that there was a certain vagueness in the question which would necessarily preclude a very definite reply, and compel the answer to be more or less general.

---

*["A third object, pursued by a portion of the members of the Society, is to investigate unexplained laws of nature and the psychical powers of man."— *Report of Proceedings, General Council, T.S.,* December, 1886]

In the first place, we consider that *all* of the Society's declared objects are together *one whole,* each important, and that we must remember that the first one having been made a condition precedent (in acceptance) to membership in the Society, it must never be lost sight of under any consideration, when the others are being pursued, inasmuch as that first object is *the raison d'être* of the Society and is the source and inward life of the Body as well as that which gives a reason — the reason held by the Masters — for pursuing either of the others. So that if a student pursues the 3^d object for his own sake or for the sake of any reward or result to be gained from the pursuit, he is in error and *not* in the right Path.

He may, and at some time must, investigate the unexplained laws of Nature and the psychical powers of man, but he is not to investigate or approach phenomena from the standpoint of Magic, which is only the outshowing of those very laws. He cannot be at one with other men until he knows these laws and understands his own nature, but as the first object *is* first because it is the important goal of his efforts, he should be sure of his motive at every step. For, the reason why those laws and phenomena are to be understood is, *not that we may perform phenomena or have psychic powers,* but in order that Universal Brotherhood may become a fact universal. No Adept at any time (except a Black one) ever became such through study of phenomena or knowledge of the laws which govern them, but because his motive for effort was to find God, or the All Wise, and to establish unity and true Brotherhood; and in that search the adepts have found the

subject of which you enquire to be of secondary importance because incidental, and yet not to be avoided, since
it constitutes a part of the great whole.

So then he who begins by the study of the phenomena
remains in the realm of phenomena, where he is surrounded by a constant and varying whirl of illusions. This
is more especially the case with those students who have
claimed in their hearts from the Law the right to advance
upon *the Path;* they more than others are surrounded by
these illusions and reached at by the subtle influences
which line the road. Such students are very likely to be
deceived and drawn into grievous trouble. The Law
and the Lodge — both being one — refuse no one. But
each must advance through the road laid down by nature,
and woe be to him if he rushes into the realm of phenomena unprepared. The needful preparation is not an
investigation of the psychical world, but purification of
heart, of speech, and of action. Hence the great Initiate
St. Paul said: "Though I speak with the tongues of men
and of angels, and know all mysteries and all knowledge,
and have not Charity, *I am nothing.*" By "Charity" he
meant love — Brotherhood, Unity; by "nothing" he meant
"powerless" — powerless to advance, powerless to avert the
final calamity sure to come from a negation of or inattention to that object found at the head of our Society's only
declarations. The great Lord Buddha declared in the
same strain when he said that a man might be able to hear
through the vast reaches of the ten points of space, or to
smell the odors denied to ordinary senses, or to see all the
grand and varied sights of the curious and unexplained

realms of Nature, *and yet not know Truth.* Why? Because these powers, principalities, and properties compose the illusory husk woven about the central Truth.

A certain phase of alleged phenomena remains to be noticed, that is, the claim that some one or other of the Masters who are behind the Society have appeared at theosophical gatherings so as to be recognized. You will perhaps recall a story recently printed in a Magazine published in Boston. In such we do not believe, and our older members, the writer among the number, concur in saying that in whatever genuine writings we have from Masters through their chosen disciples, it is clearly shown that such could not be real, but must in every instance, even where the narrators believed what they related, be a delusion and a snare. And under this head we would like to refer you to the Theosophical correspondence between Count St. Martin and Baron Liebistorf. It is our belief that Masters do not thus appear at such gatherings or any other. They do appear, we think, among men, but not with their proper form, always assuming a form which is known among Them as Their illusionary form, which would not be recognizable as that of a Master; and also that the Master does not appear to his chosen chelas even, until they have become entirely pure in heart, speech, and action. How then could They be seen by mere beginners in Theosophy, who do not even know the outer shell of themselves? For us who reverence the real Masters of whatever school such tales are not only idle, but smack a little of blasphemy against a high ideal. Further than that, such relations argue a want of even a merely intellectual knowledge of the conditions imposed in these matters, and of many things relating to Masters and their chelas which are published in various places and quite accessible. It would seem wise to be acquainted with these before hazarding acceptance of such tales or attempting trials of our own.

Fraternally yours

W Q J   Pres^t A. T. S.

P. S. Personally I can say that the foregoing expresses my sentiments and is within my knowledge.   J

———

W. R. Savage Esq   Feb. 22, 1888

My dear Sir:

I have your inquiry about position of the head in 'sleeping.'

The confusion in the different directions given by different writers arises from the fact that in all these matters *one must experiment and see what is best for oneself,* consequently each has given his own result. There is no fixed and general rule that each must follow. And so my opinion would only give you my individual experience.

In general, the head north is best; yet many are injured by it. It is the best general position for electrical and magnetic currents; the next best position is, the head east.

The best way for you is to TRY and not wait to find opinion.

Yours truly

WILLIAM Q JUDGE

P. S. Have you changed your address?

H. F. James Esq   Mar. 20 1888
Dear Sir and Bro:

You ask me what laws govern appearances of the
Brothers and for what purposes they appear in the T. S.,
and if they interfere with its organization, and how they
regard formation of Branches. This reply is not private
but should not be used with anyone piecemeal but if referred to should be shown.

You should study the probable being and constitution
of an Adept. He must be (if high) a pure man and one
who does not find it necessary to appear to impure persons.
By impure I mean not only lust but any and every sort of
fault: e.g. fault-finding, anger, bickering, self seeking, etc.
It is therefore impossible for a chela who is not thoroughly
purified to see an Adept of the character of those behind
our Society, for to see Him the chela must be able to pass
through the blaze about Him and that cannot be done
while we are in our unregenerate condition.

Sometimes the Brothers appear, but it is *very seldom*
and then only for a great purpose. As one appeared once
to Col. Olcott so as to encourage him to go on with the
great work of the T. S. the Adept knowing that he would
be the man to do the hard work. Sometimes They send
a high Chela but just as seldom. Newly pledged chelas
are not sent on trial trips that they cannot accomplish nor
for small trifling ends. The Brothers have better means
than that for bringing about their ends. Untrained trance
seers in this country (and that includes almost all) do *not*
see the Brothers but only the ideal pictures of Them that
others have formed. And those pictures *seem* alive because
they are vivified by elementals.

74

I do not believe that anyone except H. P. Blavatsky now out in the world can consciously send messages to the Brothers. I *know* from the rules laid down by the Brothers over and over again that their Chelas dare not try to approach Them for people's inquiries, wishes and objects, nor for their own. These Chelas have a work to do; they must do it under what instructions they have, *and wait 'till they are asked by the Master* before they approach Him.

The Masters of the T. S. have over and over again said that this section of it to which you and I belong is the lowest and exoteric section, and hence it is meant to give through it the light of the Masters to all men so as that they may be saved if possible. And from that lowest section ascent can be made to the others.

Do not be troubled by what others may at any time tell you Masters say on particular topics just arising: when you understand *yourself* better then you may hope to hear from Them and they require no man to be guided except by his inner voice. When he has got to hear that, then he can try further.

Fraternally yours
WILLIAM Q. JUDGE.

———

Wm. Erwin, Esq   Mar 20, 1888
Dear Sir and Bro:

Zadok and Julius request me to reply as follows to your question whether the giving up to Christ as in churches is not the same as giving up all to the Higher self, except that the first is unintelligent and the latter not?

It is not the same in effect although it springs from a similar desire. If the Higher Self is known to be the All then the difference is that Christ is not the All but a certain person — the Son of God — and therefore less than the All.

In the first case they go at death to that imaginary Christ, in the second case if the surrender is complete they go to the All which is the Higher Self. By the first, repeated experiences are needed to get to the latter which must at last be done, but by knowing the Self as the All we more quickly reach beyond death and rebirth because our meditation is toward the whole or Universals.

Fraternally

WILLIAM Q. JUDGE

———

J. Ransom Bridge Esq, F. T. S.   Mar 29, 1888.
Dear Bro. Bridge:

I have yours of 28th. We are holding over the matter referred to for No. 6.

Let us refer to the balance of yours. In the first place, although I have never intended to judge a man nor do I think I ought to, I have been before this accused of doing so. That cannot be helped as we are all mortal and I do not rebel against any one's judgment passed on me, but would wish to be able to improve under all criticism. Since we ought not to care for the applause of the world we should look within when criticised to see if we are wrong in the way the critic points out.

Now as Mr. Page has nowhere described "the way" in

which the alleged Master "made himself known" I could not, even by inference, be said to have referred to a "way" not mentioned. Nor did I refer to Mr. Page in words, and further *I* did not say anything but expressed the Branch views. Those views however are also my own. So I must deny that I have declared anyone's statements "to be false," and by rereading mine you will see that the letter very carefully said "even when the narrators believe what they say."

It is *positively laid down* by Masters and by such exponents of Theirs as H. P. Blavatsky, that They *do not* appear to any one (except for a high and noble purpose) until he has irrevocably pledged himself to Them. And the cases of "a high and noble purpose," in this inquiry, are rare.

It is therefore necessary to know who saw this alleged Master at St. Louis or where? Did only one person see? Who was that person? Were others present and if so, did they see also? Is it a report made by one person or was it an appearance to one who alone cognized and then reported? All these questions should be settled before we go to decide what the appearance was or meant. A person in a trance may report such a thing and not see a Master. A trance medium will see the pictures of Masters imagined by [you] or by me.

Then as to Olcott. *He was irrevocably pledged* to Masters and has seen Them *once*.

Mabel Collins has not yet said she saw a master. Light on the Path was precipitated; and further, you should know that high chelas do these things and appear *for* Masters but are *not* Masters. Neither of the chelas who wrote

77

"Man" has seen the Master or Masters. They saw the messengers. This I know for I know them.

Now you say "I for one try to use for a balance *the light of my own reason.*" Have you obtained yet the *facts* on which your reason is based or works regarding this question?

Please recollect I speak impersonally and that I do not wish to make a question with St. Louis or other place, but am dealing with a supposititious case. And if I am not in error when our letter was sent I had not seen the St. Louis letter.

Please say if we are to use the matter sent, in No. 6. You have not yet said.

Fraternally yours
WILLIAM Q. JUDGE

May 8th 1888

Dear Harte,

. . . . I have all yours. My dear fellow, I am not mad, not a bit. The thing that makes *me* mad is not yet known to you. I often appear "mad" to others but let me say I really am not inside in that state. Anger ruptures the cohesion of the particles that compose the inner man. If the extension was rejected, well and good. I am not the prophet of God. By the way why don't you return it to me if it was not to be used?

We are all well and busy.

No further news yet from the man and the money about Secret Doc. but I expect it every day. Distances here are enormous and time is used in waiting for trains to get in.

I omitted to say about that novel you spoke of of Hartmanns. As I have no respect for him or his novels, and as he cant write a novel I dont want to meddle in it.

Dont forget, I dont want such a load of the next reprint as you sent me of the others.

Success to you my boy. Roll on the Wheel and may the Treasure of Carnaellas be yours. If you are blown up by Jesus it is good for the soul. Ease and apathy are death.

As ever
WILLIAM Q JUDGE

Dr Thomas Docking   May 15, 1888
    San Diego, Cal.
My dear Sir and Bro,

I mailed you on Tuesday afternoon a letter closing with the remark that I would separately answer the other points in yours which arrived on Monday.

1. I do not think I can give you any useful advice as to the change of the Insurance plan. Such advice, you perceive, must be asked of me either in my capacity as a Theosophical student or in my capacity as a man of business. But in the former capacity I have no special knowledge of such matters, for Theosophy does not treat of or investigate them: it is concerned, as you know, with the distinctive problems of life and destiny, and has no especial knowledge of secular affairs. I think I may say that the most advanced

Adept would disclaim any fitness to advise in a question of this kind. Nor should I, as a man of business, have qualification to counsel you in this matter. I am a lawyer, and the problem you submit to me is not of law but of financial investment, one requiring for its solution a different class of facts and a different experience. It is almost certain, then, that advice from one without the qualifications to give value to the advice would be worthless and probably misleading. My personal opinion, however, is to keep the Insurance.

2. I do not know of any Lamasery in the States. But are you sure, my Brother, that you would better serve your own spiritual development, — to say nothing of the Cause for which we are all at work, by entering one, should it exist? I do not say that in another hemisphere and in certain special cases there may be no value in such a system. But I may safely say 2 things: 1st. that in view of the well-known effects of monastic seclusion as abundantly demonstrated in the history of monasteries, in view of the inherited and acquired temperament of one accustomed to Western life, and in view of the discipline and opportunity lost to one who withdraws from the *environment prepared for him by Karma,* an aspirant to high culture may well ask himself whether such a withdrawal might not be a mistake, and whether Krishna (in the Bhagavad Gita) was not right in urging upon Arjuna that his highest duty lay in his performance of the functions entrusted to him, NOT in the relinquishment of them: 2nd. that in a time like this, when Theosophy has received — as we believe — an impetus from Higher Powers no less wonderful than encouraging, we,

who can assist it, have immediately before us a sphere of usefulness and of good, not only to others but to ourselves in serving others, compared to which the self-culture of retirement would seem poor indeed. Upon this matter of Lamaseries I think you may find some worthy hints in Dr. Hartmann's "Adventures among the Rosicrucians," a little book published by the Occult Publishing Co. of Boston, which altho' not an account of an actual lamasery, contains many truths.

3. But even if these views were wholly erroneous, and if it could be shown beyond doubt that you were called, not only to a comtemplative life, but to admission to the "inner circle," is it clear that this should be put in the form of a "demand" and that it should be addressed to me? Are you absolutely certain that any of us know precisely the nature of this "inner circle," or what attainments give a claim to entrance therein, or when the moment has arrived when the claim can be advanced? Indeed, does not the addressing of such a "demand" to the General Secretary of the American Section of the Theosophical Society arouse a suspicion that there has been some misconception of the matter? For what is the Theosophical Society, and who its Secretary? The one is an exoteric organization with 3 declared aims, together with a no less clearly-declared disclaimer of power, as such, to communicate with Adepts or to confer spiritual gifts; the other is one of its executive officers, charged with certain oversight of its machinery. I am not an Adept; I have not, as Gen. Sec'y, any privilege of approaching Adepts; I can no more grant your "demand," or even transmit it to those who can, than can the Secretary

of your own Branch. Surely you err in your conception.

Let us look at the whole subject from another viewpoint. Bro. Syke's letter and your own account of yourself show that you have long and earnestly pursued the aims we know to be the best and highest. Let it be fully conceded that you are sincere, faithful, and a real aspirant to Wisdom. Can you believe, then, that these facts are unknown to Those whose mission it is to produce them? If not, if the Elder Brethren know and gladly hail them, do you not think that They may be trusted to fix the time and the place and the way when further light shall be given? And, if so, then it would seem that you best meet Their wishes and hasten that time by a quiet, thorough performance of every duty lying to hand, a calm assurance that you are not forgotten and will not be neglected, and a patient awaiting the initiation which their better knowledge and larger experience may perhaps deem premature as yet. I *know* that this is the way in which They tell Their personal disciples to work.

I venture these suggestions, not as an authorized expression from Higher Powers, — not at all, but simply as ideas which commend themselves as seemingly just and reasonable. If, on further thought, they so commend themselves to you, I do not think that we can be far wrong.

Very truly and fraternally yours,

WILLIAM Q. JUDGE

P. S. As I understand, in Lamaseries there [is] neither money nor the means of making it, hence in such a place you would be unable to get money to keep up your insurance.

Mrs J V Whitaker   May 15, 1888
    Boston
Madame

    . . . . Your question about sex cannot be in the Path
answered, and probably not to satisfy you, in this. Male
and female are all human beings now. The woman's body
by reason of its peculiarities makes progress in higher
occultism difficult. But it does not make it impossible, for
there are women-adepts. Again, in strict accordance with
nature, the natural character of woman is such that in the
final analysis she has a greater affinity for matter and concrete things than the male. This is a natural difference.

    The female mind — in general (there are exceptions) —
leans to concrete thought and that has a slight natural
tendency to draw her away from spirit, which is an *abstract* thing. The fact is that women are as a rule more
intuitional than men but that is not spirit. Spirit being
an abstraction it demands abstract ratiocination and as
that is not natural to women as a whole, the female
environment offers more obstruction to occultism than the
male.

    But as we are in fact neither man nor woman in occult-
ism and as bodies are only illusory the same heights can
be gained by woman as by man but with greater struggle.
Hence the ego after reaching that knowledge and after
passing through all necessary bodies to give it the required
experience strives to get a male body, or rather, naturally
gets into one which will enable it to go on easier from that
birth through many others.

    Yet also, at the same time, there are many beings in

Male bodies who are far behind women and who will not progress; and also there are many in female bodies who are in them merely working through certain experiences which will enable them to progress rapidly in this or the next life on earth whether in male or female form it matters not.

Personally I am not a disbeliever in woman, for the greatest living occultist I know is a woman — H. P. Blavatsky.

The sexes are natural divisions that cannot be evaded nor argued away and I cannot agree with you that "woman is spiritually positive." I think the reverse. Nor can I agree with you when you say "while on this earth she is negative to the immense procreative force," for you imply thus that *she*, woman, is always woman, whereas the fact is that the bodies of men and women alike are only instruments through which the real person, which is neither "she" nor "he," works out its ends in obedience to laws. Hence if the Ego escapes it escapes not as *man* or *woman* but as *soul*. It is the soul, the real, that is in the toils — either in male or female form — and not *woman* as such nor *man* as such.

The constant considering these bodies as anything but illusion is error and leads us to make arbitrary distinctions that are misleading and that bind us to earth lives.

There will always be *forms* of male and female sort to be inhabited by beings so long as the age lasts. In far distant ages, millions of years to come, other conditions will prevail perhaps, but it will make no difference to us because *we* being spirits always, will have to go through the natural material conditions, whatever they are, that prevail in any age.

You err in thinking that the knowledge you seek cannot be found in the Theosophical Society. It can be found nowhere else. And by studying theosophical writings and doctrines the true standpoint will be reached and the possibility for light to break on us be brought about.

I have stated part of the true doctrine. It will be for you to say in yourself if it is true or not. But certainly no light will be found on the sex problem or any other relating to Man until we are considered as spirits every one and until the false and illusory character of "body" removed as a conception from the mind.

ZADOK

———

18 May [1888]

Dear H P B

Please reply to this   So many people are beginning to ask me to be chelas that I must do something, so I have drawn up the enclosed paper which you can send me with some formalities on it if you think it right to do so — or whatever I ought to have. If you do not think so then please tell me in what way I had best proceed.

I know a good many good ones who will do well and who will form a rock on which the enemy will founder and this plan would encourage them. So fiat something.

As Ever

WILLIAM Q JUDGE

To William Q Judge: You are directed to draw together all those persons — members of the Theosophical Society — in the United States, who have or express the desire to serve the Cause of the Blessed Masters. This you are to do with the understanding in every case that the persons taken are not thereby made chelas of Masters but simply that they are thus given a chance to make a preliminary trial of themselves, and in each case you will take from the applicant an expression in writing, before making your private register of the name, that they will understand the basis on which you thus take them. Nothing is promised, each will have just what he or she deserves — no more no less, and all must be faithful to The Cause, to Masters and to the founders of the Theosophical Society —

Given etc. etc.

Dr. Wm Erwin   May 26 1888
    Indianolo, Iowa
Dear Sir and Bro:

Great pressure of work has prevented an earlier reply — and this is only acknowledgment.

All high aspiration is wise. But of course students should go carefully. The subject of your letter is engaging my deepest attention inasmuch as many seekers are writing the same as you have. I may soon be able to write about your earnest inner thoughts in some way that will be advisable. When I have found the proper method I will write again. Meanwhile believe me to be thinking these matters over for you, for others, and for myself.

Fraternally yours

WILLIAM Q. JUDGE

Dr. A F James   May 26, 1888
    St. Louis
Dear Sir and Bro:

Great pressure precludes the possibility of a lengthy reply to yours of 18th inst. You should read and study first Art. "Occultism and Magic Arts etc" in Lucifer for this month. It replies to you on fundamental points.

The only method of Yoga that I would give a snap for is that found in Patanjali's Yoga and the Bhagavad Gita. True Yoga is *not* autohypnotization. The true practice of yoga begins by purifying the heart; its perfection is not attainable until the personal idea is completely uprooted. Obviously this takes more than one incarnation. You have in you the Self all powerful and omniscient. It cannot act because the lower self hinders it. The hindrances must be got rid of. The way to do it is in Patanjali and Bhag. G. *It is a long, hard and awful road* — with peace at the end. All other roads lead to death. But students must measure the task and not take what they cannot do.

I may not be older than you. Age is immaterial.
                         Fraternally
                    WILLIAM Q. JUDGE

My dear Olcott   June 8, 1888

Certain matters are occurring here which need attention and action. They call, in my opinion, for definite
statements from you and from London.

What I refer to is a disposition on the part of Elliott
Coues to constantly pretend that he has power to confer
what he calls the second degree of the T. S.

If this were confined to his own immediate coterie —
as it was for a time — there would be nothing in it since
it was [would] thus remain simply ridiculous, but as he
now is gradually spreading it about and "authorizing"
persons to say that they are in such degree, and as they
are printing it, the whole thing has a tendency to cast
ridicule upon the movement and also to arouse needless
gossip and jealousy.

His policy is to place himself at the head of some
wonderful unknown thing through which (god save the
mark) communications are alleged to come from the Masters. He also in a large sense wishes to pull the T. S. away
from your jurisdiction and make himself the grand mogul
of it in this country.

Now the first thing mentioned is in itself petty but
breeds trouble. He has just got into the Religio J^{rnl} a
letter "What is Theosophy" signed Sarah Hibbert, T. S.
of 2^d degree," and this has now gone all over the country.

An authoritative statement should be made that as
yet there is no such thing permitted as "F. T. S. of 2$^{d\circ}$",
and that those who are in that degree *are bound not to
reveal it*. I intend now to send an answer to the Religio
on the subject and you as Pres^t should also.

As to the second, I know that ∴ policy is to retain complete control in you. And my desire is to keep the American Section as a dependency of the General Council in India; hence you are the Pres^t· It was never my intention to dissever, but to bind. And the form of our Constitution – about which as yet you have not uttered a word, clearly shows that. That is why no Pres^t is elected or permitted here.

C. has but lately written H P B that he must have the position permanent pres^t and he is awfully cut up that the Convention did not raise him. All he wants is to get up on our shoulders in the eyes of the people while he does not help us a bit, and none of our members want him.

So I would recommend that you call the Council and consider our Constitution, which ought long ago have been done, and decide that we are in affiliation and subordination to India and that we are recognized as a part of the general council, with power to have a secretary as a channel but not to have a yearly president but only a chairman each Convention.

Thus we will have it definite and he can do as he pleases. He has but slight influence and the sooner he gets out – if he wishes – the better for us.

Now I must ask you attend to this and not ignore it as you have the subject in general hitherto.

I speak from facts, for I now know *all* our 500 members. I know who they are, what they want and who they follow.

Have you sent Coues any charters? He says you have. If so they should be called in.

If you treat this as you have in the past similar matters then I shall not be held responsible, for I cannot work this thing here properly without your cooperation.

As Ever

WILLIAM Q JUDGE

My dear Tookaram: June 16, 1888

. . . . The letter from Khandalavalla and as was printed by me as you see by Path. That ends the matter as I wish to avoid controversy. It is delightful to find you working staunchly *"with no hope of reward"* for the cause we love, and I trust you will not be moved from that attitude. The "Secret Doctrine" is coming out here and in London by Nov and thus all disputes may end. "Offences will come but woe to him by whom they come" must still be true. The T. S. has great strength in America; and the defection from its ranks in India or Europe of a few will not affect us here. I believe the T. S. is now passing through a certain stage in which the *real characters of all prominent F. T. S. are to be unveiled,* and until that is over much silence will prevail from the Masters.

Fullerton was glad to get your good wishes. He is doing great good here. Please remember me to Rustanji and all others,

and believe me,

As Ever yours

WILLIAM Q JUDGE

Samuel E. Horton, Esq.   June 18 1888
   Washington D C
Dear Sir:
   I have yours of 15th in which you offer me a biographical sketch of Dr. E. Coues for the Path at $50., to fill one issue. I am obliged to decline your kind offer, as I have never yet paid money for anything printed in the Path and never shall probably. And besides your sketch is too long. I was only able to devote 4 pages to Col. Olcott, who with myself and Mme Blavatsky founded the Society, and of course could hardly go beyond that in dealing with younger members however scientific and famous they may be.
   Hoping you may dispose of your MS. elsewhere,
             I am, truly yours,
                   WILLIAM Q JUDGE

———

                                          June 18, 1888
Miss Laura Charles
   The misunderstanding, if any, is easily explained.
   In your first letter you said that your friend assured you that you had *entered the silence* and found the *peace,* spoken of in Light on the Path, while in your writing you showed a troubled condition which negatived the idea of that peace having been attained. The silence and the peace spoken of in that book are very advanced conditions, and while I could not deny any person's assertion that

they had reached that, yet when you asked me and furnished in your letter evidence that it had not been reached I answered as I did.

The question you asked, to which I replied "yes," was whether by striving and continuing you would reach the goal desired. This seemed also the burden of your thoughts and therefore I did not suppose I needed to repeat your statement of it. When we make the first step and are determined to continue then it contains in it the fulfillment of our desires, for each further step grows out of the first one. Hence in India they say that he who earnestly reaches the first stage has reached salvation because that genuine impulse will one day bring him to the Truth.

This letter is in my handwriting. The other I directed written, and then added to it before sending. I shall be happy to help you at any time if I can, and when you go away hope that you will send your new address.

I thank you for your donation, but as your subscription to Path has expired I would like to know if the money shall not be applied to a renewal.

Yours truly
WILLIAM Q JUDGE

Mrs. Mary Frances Wight,   June 26, 1888
Dear Madame:

I have yours of 23$^{d.}$ My previous letter to which you take exception and in which you say there is a lack of fraternal recognition, was one merely of acknowledgment of the receipt of yours. The rules under which I have been educated require that I should not enter into discussion of matters personal to myself and that I should not attempt exculpation either. This letter for the same reason, must also remain as one that is solely in acknowledgment of yours.

Fraternally yours,
WILLIAM Q. JUDGE.

————

Chas H Whitaker Esq June 30, 1888
Dear Sir:

I have yours of the 28th. No *form* of ritual has ever been adopted by the T. S. Councils. The only authorized method — which is not a ritual — is, to give the candidate the signs and passwords properly explaining them at the same time. Any ritual which is used at the time is of course only meant by the Branch using it to be a means of impressing the signs and passwords on the mind of the person. The ritual which was spread by the Rochester Branch was made up by a free-mason of this city. The proper way was exemplified at the Chicago Convention where one of your members, Bro. Stearns, was present.

At the same time all Branches are at liberty to use a ritual in addition if they see fit, and if they carefully inform the candidate that it is their own and that the theosophical method of communicating for the purposes of recognition is by the use of the signs etc, and that the *ritual* is not that of the T. S. as a whole.

Hence it follows that, if a Branch President has a member at large to initiate he must in his case, use no ritual but merely give and explain the signs and passwords: the ritual is to be reserved for members taken into the Branch. This seems clear and easy. I had no intention of dictating and only stated facts in my other letter as they existed. Personally I would not care to use the Rochester Ritual considering the attitude and words of Mrs. Cables about the T. S., its founders, and the fact that Mr. Bowen who actively helped her has gone into the Roman Catholic Church and has slandered Mme. Blavatsky and others very shamefully. Then again two years or so ago the initiation as a means of becoming a member of T. S. was done away with and it was decided in India to leave entrance merely to application and endorsement followed by election, the signs and passwords to be for recognition only.

If Mr. Winter should apply to you, you will initiate him in the manner above indicated. I admit that it would be advisable to have a general scheme of explanation of signs etc adopted uniformly among the Branches; and it will no doubt be accomplished.

2 vols. of Sec. Doct. complete all that will now come out and not five. Any other vol. will be additional. The 3d vol. is of practical magic and will not, I think be issued, since neither English nor American people are ready for it but might drop into Black Magic!

Fraternally

WILLIAM Q JUDGE

Dear Mrs. McPherson:

I have your letter which I have carefully read, and have sent it to a coworker of ours who is a lady not only of refinement but also of very deep intuition in Theosophical matters, asking her to write you. As she is a woman she can at present help you better than I can and will gladly do it.

I think the class *is* an opportunity. As you say it is not easy to know when to speak. But right speech comes to us if we are deeply in earnest and feel our own ignorance. No one person can answer all the questions that are asked, nor would a year suffice. Hence you can make general answers and refer to Karma and Reincarnation and above all to the doctrine of the Unity of Spirit. It is all in fact the thing that Jesus taught if we leave out the idea of vicarious atonement and that he alone is God's son. We are all potentially that.

I would advise you to leave lying about various theosophical books and papers. They will excite questions and often also answer them; and I would *think* of the people also. In that way the sincere will ask you and you can pass them on. I send you for the purpose some printed matter.

I thank you for your kind thoughts and expressions.

Sincerely yours

WILLIAM Q JUDGE

In helping others you will be helped yourself.

Dr. J. M. Borglum   July 4 1888
    Omaha
Dear Sir and Bro.

Thanks for the little poem. I will lay it aside for future use.

I think while we acquire a distaste for the things of the world we should also endeavor to realize how much help poor humanity needs, struggling as people are in the mire of illusion and false creeds. As humanity needs our help we must therefore work with it. Not in formulating new schemes for temporary good, for all those political, social and labor problems are merely for the moment. They solve nothing since the cause of sorrow remains. But they will be pushed by their different votaries. We as theosophists know that the real remedy lies in true views of man's nature and destiny. As we are here in the world and as there is no one else save Man to be helped, and as we cannot separate ourselves from our fellows because we too helped to make up this mass of bad Karma, we must learn to sympathise with these people and not shrink from them, trying to turn their attention to the mighty truths given out by The Masters. This is what Masters desire us to do above all else. They do not seek for mere occultists and adepts but for men who are willing to work for the sacred cause of Humanity. The laborer truly is downtrodden, the rich are also, but each really treads on himself; and nothing but belief in Karma and good living on a basis of Brotherhood will cure the evil. I shall at any time be glad to hear from you.

                              Sincerely yours
                              WILLIAM Q JUDGE

My dear Foulke: July 9, 1888

The enclosed are letter and telegram sent on 6th to all Branches West. Responses already from California and Nebraska are: "*cordial support to Mme Blavatsky in everything.*"

This is the 9th month of our 13th year as a Society and the crisis *has* come. It is in India and really with the Council and not with Col. Olcott. Mme Blavatsky ought to be the head west of Bombay shore and this action is needed to show them that, and to show them that they do not know the needs of the West. Mme Blavatsky has been ordered to take this step and as she is really the life of the T. S. as a whole her request should be acceded to. There exist in certain places psychic currents that if not broken will do harm to parts of the organization at a distance. Hence although the crisis does not show *here* it is nevertheless existent and important. As she is our real head and represents the Masters we ought to do as she asks, for if she is not such head then we are like any other organization. The sooner this is shown one way or the other, the better. She has months ago warned me of this crisis and I hope you will call a meeting at once and give assent. Good results will follow.

As Ever

WILLIAM Q JUDGE

Dear Mrs. Savery   July 10 1888

I was so very busy that Mr. Fullerton merely acknowledged yours. There is no very great news theosophically. Things are going forward. The Secret Doctrine will probably be out in the fall.

I have taken an additional room at 117 Nassau St which will be devoted to a Theosophical Headquarters and be open all day. Mr. Fullerton being always here makes this feasible. But I will want some little furniture, as, chairs, rugs, table etc, and if you can spare any articles of that sort and donate them to the room it will greatly help. The room will be useful, as many people call, and more will come when this place is open. I will have Indian pictures and various other things, and a line shields along the wall near the ceiling for the names and date of founding each U. S. Branch. Dont you think the idea good? We will also have theos. and other cranky magazines.

Very sincerely

WILLIAM Q JUDGE

———

Dr. T. Docking,   July 10, 1888
    San Diego Cal
Dear Sir and Bro:

I have your letter enclosing papers about Dr. Babbitt and will give the matter attention. Just at present I am very busy and cannot for a few days look over the article sent. I shall soon send you something for the P. L. L.

[Point Loma Lodge]. But I can say now that one should not confine others to any one method, for when many persons come together there is always diversity of view which is healthy. Some order of procedure should be adopted which will meet best the views of all and all should agree that no one person's views only can prevail. There ought to be some candid discussion of philosophy and comparison of views — not debate, but calm discussion. Accepted Chelas have to learn in that way, by coming together and comparing views and occurrences with the object of deducing from the accumulated experience the laws which govern. In that way they progress. They meditate privately. And each Branch should regularly study such books as Bhagavad Gita and Raj Yoga Philosophy, the views of all being heard, so that the whole Lodge may as a Unit proceed upon the same road. — I was glad to get your telegram so promptly. On 16th I shall report all to Mme B.

Hastily yours
WILLIAM Q JUDGE

———

New York, July 11, 1888

Dear Mrs. Brainard:

I received yours in reply to my question about Isis and the ☆ pointed star and have looked at the reference given. I do not think that the statement made on p. 448 is an allusion which supports in any way the position taken by you.

At p. 448 the author is speaking of the star of Lucifer

in his aspect of "Devil," and then it is always made with the point down; and the context shows that this is so, for it distinctly shows the 5 pointed star to be "the murderer's" star. When the same star is written with the point up it then is the star of good, white-magic as shown in E Lévi and elsewhere. What Hartmann says on the subject is not of much consequence as he merely copies others.

Inasmuch as the star may be written in either way, and that one way means life and the other death, it does not appear that there is any error or confusion in "Isis."

Fraternally yours,
WILLIAM Q. JUDGE

———

My dear Page,

July 11th, 1888

You are altogether right in supposing that the request in the telegram comes from Madame Blavatsky herself, for the Lodge called after her name has no authority over us and would instantly disclaim any.

No, there is no falling out between the Founders, and, I am confident, never will be any. Indeed, a letter just received by me from Col. Olcott shows the contrary.

Briefly, the facts are these. Col. O. has in Adyar an Executive Committee of 7. Of these, 4 have for some time lost interest in him and faith in Madame. It has been found that some of them have been circulating belittling tales against her, arousing distrust and ill-feeling, and imperiling the whole work of the T. S. A crisis has been approaching, and it was precipitated by the official request from a large number of Branches for a distinct statement from Headquarters as to the loyalty or otherwise of this Executive Committee. The last "Theosophist" announces the resignations of Subba Row and Dr. Cooke.

Experience, and the existence of certain complications too long now to detail, show the need of having all the Western Branches under the more immediate supervision of Madame B, the whole Theosophical Society remaining, of course, under the presidency of Col. O, the President-Founder. Under instructions, as I have reason to believe, of the Higher Powers behind the T. S., Madame has determined to assume this subordinate and localized leadership, i.e. of all Branches in Europe and America, — all, in short, west of India. Fortified by their request and assurance of support, she can say to the President, "You see the response called forth by the disloyalty and the slanders of those whom you and I trusted in the Executive Committee. They are no more true to you than to me. If, as is probable, they oppose your consent to my taking this subordinate leadership in the West, you can exhibit to them my Western endorsement as proof that their hostility is combated and will be overborne by the West. This will enable you to resist their opposition to my course, a course inspired by Those higher than either of us, strengthen your hands against these unfaithful ones, and pave the way for a reconstruction of the Committee from sincere and trustworthy Councillors."

Col. O. has no better friend than Madame B, and she sees, even more clearly than any of us here, how essential it is to his interests and to those of the whole T. S. that the Council should be purged of secret enemies and their places filled by friends. In his isolated position he needs support, and she, instigated by the Wise Ones, asks us to give it. My confidence in her and in Them is intense, and I at once sent the telegrams as she desired.

Ever yours faithfully,
WILLIAM Q JUDGE

July 12 1888

Dear Coues:

I have yours and I take it in the spirit in which it was written, *but* you have misunderstood. Please observe that neither as Aryan Pres^t nor as Gen. Sec. have I asked any Branch to do anything whatever hence the major part of yours relating to the impropriety of my attempting to do so does not apply. And my letter in blue printing had *no heading* and is *signed as an individual* and expressly states that representing H. P. B. I ask them to consider what she proposes. The same was sent to every Branch and none have the slightest proof that I acted otherwise than as an individual agent for H. P. B.

I would not make the request as Sec. nor propose it to the Ex Com nor as CCC for the simple and easy reason that H. P. B. on Friday by telegraph ordered me to do what I did. And when she orders me I do as she says without reasons. At some expense I telegraphed you fully the very first person, and as yet you give no reply for Gnostic that is official. Have you cabled H P B yourself that Gnostic is in the affirmative? If you have that is all I care. *The T. S. is H. P. B.* and hence what she wishes done should be; so you have not come up to the measure laid down by yourself. This matter is wholly and solely H. P. B. and no one else and the outcome is hers. I had no information. The cable came Friday bald and bare, and my request was wired Saturday to every Branch. Had I had information I would have consulted you. Since then I have a letter notifying me that a circular letter from H. P. B. will come here. When it does we may and will act officially upon it, and when I telegraph you about it I hope you will early reply. There is a crisis which no one but H. P. B. can use and avert and pass. It will be for the best. But its details I do not yet know. I send you herein my cable from her which please return.

I intended to call the Hdqrs Aryan but they shall be devoted by Aryan to general use and benefit of T. S., and I followed your request in notifying you so that if you wanted more buncombe in it you might have it.

Your remarks that I might by consultation have even little whims carried out by Com and CCC are noted and my old reply is repeated that I shall never ask either body for authority or countenance for anything like whim nor for aught but regular routine matter.

There is no split with H. S. O. but I believe the whole

affair of H. P. B.'s telegram is to work on the asinine Council H. S. O. has about him in India.

Do not forget photo soon as I am collecting and arranging everything now.

As Ever

WILLIAM Q JUDGE

P. S. I have received telegraphic and written replies from All T. S. Branches but 3 that they have passed the resolution *nem con.* Among the 3 I do not count Gn. Rochester is nix of course, and by Sunday I will have all. Monday shall cable full report to H. P. B.

Dear H. P. B.   July 13 1888

As before said I notified all Branches of your resolution for vote. Replies as follows: I telegraph'd you on 16th. Cost so far is $30. or £ 6. the telegram of 16th additional at 12 cents a word.

Affirmative on resolution:

Chicago two branches;
Cincinnati
Philadelphia
New York
Grand Island, Nebraska   12 in all
St. Louis (one) "Pranava"
Bridgeport, Conn.
Pt. Loma, California
Santa Cruz, California
Lotus, Mich. conditional, if within the rules.
Gnostic, D. C., not official: in letter from C.

No reports yet
San Francisco   Rochester nor ever
Los Angeles

No report

Boston, and Malden, Mass ⎫
Iswara, Minn.   ⎪
Omaha, Neb.   ⎬ 8 in all
Arjuna, St. L.   ⎭

Against

Esh Maaûn, St. Louis, because "in the dark" and dont know why or what is about.

Effect all over U. S. Branches.
So far, *bad.*

Reason for effect.
No Branch knows of any difficulty with Olcott or any one else; some know about Paris racket.   They hence are filled with, (a) idea that there is a split with Olcott, (b) idea that it is now at a head and must be dreadful, (c) distrust because of want of information as to why all the bother.

The Paris, India, and London rows may make trouble in those several places but they are not heard of, *nor cared for* over here.   Even I do not know much either and have to guess at a good deal by intuition.   The Isis Bulletin makes a fair show, but of course is only *one side* and there is a maxim: *Audi alterum partem.*   As Corresponding Sec. out of Council you had no official right to annul the Charter.   If done by petition to Council it would have weight.   Gaboriau is an ass anyhow and conceited. But what you do with T. S. even if it be to burst it up must be O. K. If it is not fit to go on, the sooner I know it the better for me. So whatever you do although my sense of diplomacy and of regularity is against it — is acceptable.

Fullerton sends his homages to you and begs you to consider him your servant.

Wouldn't it be well to give me some light on this crisis?

As Ever the same

WILLIAM Q JUDGE

P. S. Coues berates me like a pickpocket for sending those telegrams, but I dont care.

————

Dear H. P. B.   14 July 1888

One of your many devotees has put in my hands $23.00 for your private expenses. Don't ask any questions but simply put it in your privy purse.

Ever

WILLIAM Q JUDGE

————

Dear Bro Bennet,   July 16, 1888

I received your long letter and you must excuse a short reply as I am so busy.

If you carefully observe my communications by mail and telegraph regarding the "crisis" you will see that I carefully wrote as a private person and not as Gen. Sec., and as representing H. P. Blavatsky the individual. You will also see that a distinction was made between Olcott as President and Olcott as an individual. The President (H. S. O.) might have, under orders of Council to do what, as Col. Olcott, he would not like to do. So the resolution may be a slap in the face of the President and yet not in the face of *Col.* O. an individual. H. P. B. is the T. S. and without her it is absolutely nothing. She requested me to ask this and I did so. At present I have no more information, but she cannot do what will harm the T. S.; on the contrary I believe the result will be for general good.

When she writes me, as no doubt she will, I shall at once inform you.

> Fraternally yours
> WILLIAM Q JUDGE.

———

New York, July 21 1888

Dear Keightley

I got your nice long letter. I also, so busy and rushed, have not had time to write you, but I still love you and think of you. Mrs. Judge has been sick for 3 weeks but is better and now as she gets well the old man Smith is again sick. The stones, doors and windows of decaying houses flap, fall out and yawn before the final determination of the house's period.

I am sure I do not know what is to do with T. S. If it still is the visible agent of ∴ then no harm can come for at the last moment They will save it — so They said to me two years ago. H P B is mysterious you know for good reasons of her own. You may bet that the rows and talks on the surface never mean much and only are a cover for real work underneath for she always has *something to do*. So now when something important is on we cannot find out anything. Therefore we all *stick* to her. It looks from the outside bad, because H S O will not agree to her demand. If she does the ridiculous thing Harte tells me in a recent letter then it will be worse. But I never found her doing a ridiculous thing where the real interests of the T. S. lay. I was directed to work with Coues on *condition that he trusted me and reciprocated*. But he is false and has lately tried to get a paper from H S O without telling me, in which he failed. Hence there can be no trust or confidence. If he is given *any* office he will make it supremely ridiculous and keep it for his private use. Still They know who to use and how: and I do not. So I will plunge ahead and follow H P B even to a total burst up of T. S. For me the T. S. is H P B and .˙. and so if they say "disintegrate" I say the same. H S O will blow me to Hades for the crisis telegrams but I am sure I dont care. He has a big Socy and a library and a fund that no one gets any good out of and I think he rather leans to keeping the T. S. as it is. Still he is devoted and will do what he ought at the last moment for he like us is O without H. P. B. and he knows it too.

I have taken the next room to Path and fitted it up — sparsely — as a T. S. hdqrs — as a beginning. I will fill it with idols and barbarian smells so as to strike awe to

108

the visiting beholder. Hope to see it result in something bigger and better. Call and see it.

You must have a fine time over there. But I dont pity you much as you can stand it. Still, dont get strained. I pity Harte, he is such a moaner.

All send regards

As Ever

WILLIAM Q JUDGE

July 24, 1888

My dear Olcott

I have yours in which you ask for a certificate of your admission to the bar. I enclose the desired certificate, cost $1.00. You can add it to what you owe for the speaking tubes or you can call it quits. If you have already remitted for the mouthpieces you need not bother about this, as it is too small.

I am glad you are at last going to take some proper notice of the Convention. If notice had been taken before of U. S. affairs it would perhaps have been better. There is no doubt that American T. S. affairs are looking up; and I — perhaps alone — regard the U. S. as the centre of the movement, for I believe that it is here the next race will appear. It is significant that the T. S. was started here. India is necessary to it, as I said in Path, and it to India. But India cannot claim to be it all. Indeed it is getting to be secondary I think, even if the Adepts still reside there. I am fully in accord with you as to the

109

importance of the Library and all the rest, but I want to suggest that the T. S. if it is what it claims, a thing of ∴ creation, cannot remain where it was when it was started or where it got to in 1884. It must press on, and it must change or — it must die. Hence a change is expected in its 14th year which is heralded and felt to begin in its 13th. This is the 13th year and this will witness a change. I do not know if you are ready to meet it. It has seemed to me that you have of late got a fondness for forms; and I have always thought that you *gave away* your power to Boards and committees too much. Your idea that the T. S. must be put into such a shape that it might live on after your death is based upon the assumption that you are the only man who could carry it on and that at your death it would die unless its rules and constitution were fixed. This I do not concur in. If you died, some others would be provided. The T. S. is getting stuck and it has to be got out of the rut. Of course these are only my opinions.

What are the slang phrases that you notice in the Report and the Path? I know of none but if pointed out would be glad. It may happen that some expressions called slang by the Anglo Indian are not so regarded here.

I telegraphed you about Coues. All the same, as I have for 2 years kept you well informed about him, it seemed as if you could have decided yourself. Besides, such an act would be against your own forms.

As Ever

WILLIAM Q

Am glad S. R. et al are out. They are N. G.

To W. S. Wing F. T. S. Esq   24 July 1888
    Omaha
Dear Wing

. . . . I think you are in a good position. When a man gets where he can say that he knows his own unfitness or that he knows nothing, he is in a good position. Generally men assume that they are fitted for anything and good enough. This is because they do not — generally *will* not — understand the requisites demanded by the great Law and the Lodge, and then after a while they are disappointed and say they are deceived. Therefore you have got beyond this possibility.

Still I fear you have perhaps a wrong view in another matter. You say you want the truth, and that you will do anything to get it. Now the Truth is always with us, and no one holds us back from it but ourselves.

Hence if one wants the truth, his first step must be taken, not *outside* but inside of himself. And no act or deed of either suffering or heroism will give us the truth nor the right to it, until one has himself become porous so to speak to truth — open to it — so that we ourselves know.

Obviously therefore one has to change his entire nature, and that has to be accomplished gradually. The first step is to get into your attitude: the truth is not got at once. If therefore a man is determined to seek truth, the first step taken holds the possibility of the very last. I will write you again — write me.

Fraternally

WILLIAM Q JUDGE

Dearest Keightley   Aug 16 1888

Yours at hand. I am officially in the mtn's, actually
here for a day. Much obliged for your newsy letter. Wish
I had it viva voce from you. Do send me copy of all that
your bedevilled stenographer takes down. I can make
lots of the least of it. I want the clear report and make
my own explanations.

Am glad you are in charge. Keep the business tight
from Occultism and theosophy. They dont mix and the
trouble has been that they have hitherto been mixed.

Do you really believe H S O is coming? I dont. He
writes me July 14 and dont refer to it. He says he hopes *to
force* Europe to Convene and have organization like Amer.
Sec! Theres your chance take it call a convention and
put Gen Secy and Pres^t in London. Make H P B Pres^t of
European Section. Notify L. L. Blv L. Dub L Paris* etc
etc you have the votes. If you do it and they dont respond
why then form it with what you do get. By management
you can get Johnston and certainly Paris. Let L. L. slide
if it desire. Those are my sentiments. Bus!

As I am in awful hurry for train I must close and ask
you to excuse these ancient sandstone bird tracks. My
love to all and my blessing rest on your Theosophical
heads and especially the liver. The latter is an important
organ.
                        As Ever
                    WILLIAM Q JUDGE

* [London Lodge, Blavatsky Lodge, Dublin Lodge, Paris Lodge, etc.]

112

Dear Harte: Aug 16, 1888

I have yours of Aug. 4th . . .

I dont know Mrs. Galindo from Adam. I hope her paper will not be full of error of any sort.

Nirmanakaya. It is old. H. P. B. has written of it before in the Theos^t· It is a fact; but it dont explain all that you refer to. Certainly it does not have to be mixed up with shells etc. Persons a short time in Kama L (except Suicides and wicked) do not have to do with the problem, Sinnett to the contrary. No *one* explanation will do for phenomena. I dont believe Sylphs etc have to do with Séances except as agents — call them Elem^tals· They have to do with every séance. I dont see that it is mixed. Nirmanakaya is for totally different purposes.

Glad they have the stenographer. I would like to be there. What's this about H. S. O. I dont believe he is coming at all. Did H. P. B. say so. He writes me July 14 and doesnt refer to it. Hence I care not. If did 'twould do no good. H S O and I are as different in idea and temperament as onions and squash. Take your choice.

Have been away a week and return again to mtn's today for another. All the London theosophists should be duly spanked. Keep your courage and dont mix oil and water unless you have a mediator.

As Ever yours
WILLIAM Q JUDGE

113

Ctsse C Wachtmeister   Aug 25, 1888
    London
My dear Friend:
    I have your kind letter. I would like to write for the
T. P. S. other matter, but am too busy. Were you here
and could see the load I have to carry you would wonder
how I do anything. This I say merely as a fact. The
work gets done though by some power beyond me. It is
not possible to write well under such a strain on a subject
that you have * in mind. My correspondence is enormous, and if Bro. Fullerton were not helping I would
simply throw into the waste basket some 3 pounds of
correspondence per day. Since Harte was here the work
has increased 7 fold. We are free from the turmoil you
experience in London and in that respect are fortunate,
and yet you are fortunate in that you are all so near the
extraordinary person who seems to cause the whirlpool
although she does not. It is the whirling water that makes
a whirlpool and not the rock around which it rushes.
    Lucifer's last no. of Vol. 1 ends the year in a blaze of
glory. It is a good no. Am glad that Blossom and Fruit
is ended and fitly so in the grinning skull of a corpse. On
the lines adopted by the writer the career of Fleta could
not have been chronicled in five incarnations.
    Our little T. S. hd'qrs here is quite a success. Can you
not send me your photograph for the Album?
    I had hoped to meet Olcott in London and have the
pleasure of seeing you all, but the fates are presently
against it.   Sincerely yours
  * indecipherable   WILLIAM Q JUDGE
114

Dr. J. M. Borglum   Aug. 31, 1888
   Omaha, Neb.
Dear Sir and Bro:
   I duly received the book from you which I lent to Bro Wing. I am glad to hear that it has been of service to you: it has done me good also. As you say, the road to truth is at times very hard, but the resolute man can accomplish the work if he only keeps at it, but we should not forget that the great enemy — nature — is always ready to prevent us, even up to the gate of peace.
As ever sincerely yours,
WILLIAM Q JUDGE

Mrs. L M McCann   Aug 31, 1888
   Santa Cruz Cal.
Dear Madame:
   . . . . Regarding psychic development asked of by you. Our 3ᵈ object is *not* the *development* of psychic power, it is the *investigation* of it. At the same time the doctrines and philosophy of the T. S. give explanations of the psychic facts all about us. The only book I can recommend is Patanjali's Yoga Philosophy. People who come in to the T. S. desiring phenomena will be disappointed and will leave. Such is my experience. The T. S. is meant for a great reform and not for the helping of people to be clairvoyant, etc. Patient and earnest seekers come to the conclusion that all the phenomena are wonderful illusions of other planes and that they lead directly away from

spirit; and also that mediumistic or spiritualistic doings are distinctly injurious to *both the living and the dead.*

In July Path is an article "Culture of Concentration" which, if studied, will give the Key to a great deal of this question, and if Patanjali is studied and *practised* success will ensue. But a phenomena hunting is selfishness and leads to failure. If one leaves spiritualism and attempts the practise of Occultism he enters a hard and dangerous Path and leaves a path (that of Spiritualism) which while not hard is injurious because it obstructs the souls *real* advance, and alluring because full of pleasant mirages. This at least is what I think. Many thanks for your photo. Can you get me some of your members?

Sincerely yours
WILLIAM Q JUDGE

J Ransom Bridge Esq   Aug. 31, 1888.
   Boston.

My Dear Bridge:

As I was away in the country I have been unable to reply to yours. The affair you refer to is now long in the past and time rushes in this part of the cycle with amazing rapidity. I did not look at it as "utter submission" at the feet of H P B at all. She is not an "instrument" only but is at the same time a great deal more, but what and how much more each one has to find out for himself. He who finds out early is the better off, but at the same time he

116

who does not find out is not blamed — he is merely a loser. It is a thing that I cannot explain in a letter. When she is dead then perhaps it will be better known but even then not to a great many. At the same time as she is the founder of the T S it has always seemed to me that what she asks to be done ought to be done. And I have never and do not now agree to the statements so often made by those who do not know that she has "made mistakes": I do not think that she has made any and I do not think that there [is] any member in the Society who has the knowledge to be able to judge in the matter of her actions or so-called mistakes. It is not at all like the pope. But in these matters each one must judge for himself and he is not informed of any consequences or penalties for refusal: he is only asked to say yes or no.

Ever Sincerely yours,
WILLIAM Q JUDGE

———

Dear Bro. Hoisington: Aug. 31, 1888.

I do not know if that sermon was ever preached or not. I will try and find out for you. It is not impossible.

There are many errors in "Esoteric Buddhism" and perhaps this is one of them to which you refer. I am writing this at home and have not the Epitome at hand. It is my opinion that the chain of planets is a different thing from what Sinnett supposed. He was giving out a thing that was strange to him then, and fell into a lot of errors, but in the main he is correct, and I am now giving you the opinion of Mme Blavatsky on the value of his book. It is of the greatest value and we must thank him for what he has done. He is not now in the same frame of mind, but has come to think that he can determine the mystery that is forever about Blavatsky.

Ever Sincerely Yours,

WILLIAM Q. JUDGE

———

Box 2659

N. Y. Sep 1 1888.

Madame A. C. Rasche
  University of Va., Va.
Dear Madame:

Your letter remained unanswered in consequence of my absence on vacation.

I could not reply to yours fully in one letter as the subject of Karma is too great. "Karma" is not only a law that governs us but is also used to designate the operations of the law and also the facts and circumstances of life. It also means action of any kind. You see therefore that is a word of very wide significance, and that it should not be limited in any way. It is The Law. The Universe is called also Karma. The word used to designate the lesser operation of law is the word *Dharma* which also means religion and duty in the widest aspect. As, it is the *dharma,* or duty, or law, of fire to burn.

Sincerely yours

WILLIAM Q JUDGE

Dr. W. P. Phelon   Sep. 19 1888
    Chicago
Dear Phelon:
    Much obliged. Am glad to tell you all I know. Olcott
is in London to try and get up a European council on our
plan, and himself needs the request from America to make
H. P. B. head West of India, in order to back him up with
his blessed Adyar Council. Hence these tears and re-
quests. You see the U. S. is now strong and its voice
counts for something in either war or peace. The resolution affects not us and merely asks that H. P. B. be *declared* to be what she really always was. She intends
nothing here just now except to always help us, but has
a design to better the European status. I have heard
from there within a week and know that the above gives
the exact thing. Olcott has a desk beside her now and
they are in complete accord.
    Bro. Harte, one of my old members, goes to India on
the 20th to be beside H. S. O. there and to help him in his
manifold labors. That makes the 3d from N Y not count-
ing me who planned to go but whom circumstances prevented.
    Regards to Mrs. Phelon
                        As Ever
                        WILLIAM Q JUDGE

Miss Mary E. Comstock,   Sep. 19, 1888
    New York
    Your interesting letter of today (dated 20) is at hand.
Am sorry you have been so bothered by the formalities,
but think all can be smoothed out.

    It would probably be unwise to see the persons named,
except perhaps Mrs Longstreet whom I know slightly.
Perhaps if you can call here at the T. S. Hdqrs No 117
Nassau St, Room 45-46 and see me the matter of the application can be arranged. I am generally here at 9 a.m.
but can meet you at some other hour, say 1. And in my
absence Mr. Fullerton is always here. The Hdqrs are for
inquirers as well as theosophists, and you will be welcome.

    As to Mrs. Longstreet's sapient advice, I may say that
no society can benefit one who will not work in it, since
coöperation demands effort from all. If one is working
in it for his or her own salvation there is not much benefit
either. And in Theosophy especially the benefit comes
from unselfish effort and is not conferred in exchange for
dues nor to those who sit calmly with mouths open. The
"great teacher" you speak of was a simple Calcutta hindu,
one of the thousands of Bengali babus to be found there.

    Hoping to see you, I am, yours truly

WILLIAM Q JUDGE

My dear Doctor:

I must apologize to you for short letters, but the fact is that I have a very large official and business correspondence and so cannot devote as much time to my friends as I would wish; then there are many of the questions already answered in the Path, and for that reason it is not necessary to go all over the ground again. Indeed I may say that all the articles in the Path are written to be read carefully and more than once. I do not think that a man can hope to attain the full perfection of concentration in this bustle, but that is no reason for not trying to get as much as our nature and the circumstances in which we live will permit. For if a beginning is not made the struggle is only put off to a later life, whereas if we do something towards it now as best we can then so much is gained for the next earth life — we are thus so much ahead.

The fact that we are born in this kind of a place and time shows that that is our karma and it is our duty to make the most of it for if we win to any extent in such difficult circumstances then we have acquired more actual strength than if it had been our fortune to be born in a nation or time which to our short sight seems a better fortune. But it is a mistake for a man to ever suppose that any other sort of fortune than the one that is now his is a better one; that which is now ours is the best because it is the only one that by any possibility could be ours, and if we long for any other we commit a grave error and give ourselves trouble in the future, for we set up certain tendencies that MUST at some time be overcome. By working out our duty with a single heart we unconsciously acquire a large degree of concentration. I hope I am clear.

Sincerely yours
WILLIAM Q JUDGE

Miss Mary Musaeus   Sept 28, 1888
    Washington D C
Dear Madame:

I have read with care your letter and that of Mr. Higgins, and return the latter.

In my capacity as General Secretary I only deal with the exoteric business of the Society, and that is so onerous that I have but little time to write about such an important matter as chelaship, yet as you have done me the honor to address me on the subject I have to reply.

I have no authority to take pledges from would be chelas, and know of no one who can speak with authority on that subject outside of Madame Blavatsky. Chelaship is an affair of the inner nature and not a thing about which one can apply to an office or to such a person as myself. The "accepted chela" is one whom no one knows save the Master, and to become one often takes many incarnations of ceaseless effort for the good of others. Hence it follows that to aspire to that without having performed those actions and developed that character which ensures acceptance is a wrong position to assume. I do not judge however, that you have not performed those actions and at-

122

tained that development. Sages like the Masters cannot "accept" mere aspirations for the simple reason that the latter still are living on a plane of development so much lower than the Master that there is a natural barrier, the same that prevents the child under a preparatory master from being instructed by the head professor.

I ask your perusal of the article entitled To Aspirants in the copy of Path now sent you. It is all true; and you and Mr. Higgins are not alone in your desire. It is supposed that the work of merely preparing oneself for being a mere chela on probation takes many years. That effort and work you can make and do, for none can be refused or prevented. *But it must be made.* The rules formulated after the experience of thousands of centuries cannot be broken for the aspirations of the most devoted person.

May I ask if you and Mr. Higgins are members of the Theosophical Society?

Sincerely yours
WILLIAM Q JUDGE

Mary B. Horton   Box 2659, N. Y., Sep. 29, 1888
   Los Angeles
Dear Madame:

Your letter in regard of Mr. X—— came duly to hand.

You say that he was "virtually expelled" before the action of the Branch was had. Expulsion is something which cannot be virtual, it must be actual.

In this case there has been committed a very grave irregularity such as would not stand in any society whatever, let alone in ours. The member was expelled as the record sent me by the President shows without notice and without a trial; for a trial which takes place in the absence of the accused and without notice to him is no trial, and indeed there is no accused person either unless the charges have been given to him. This was not done in the present case. If it should stand it would be our first and most dangerous precedent. I am not now announcing any decision but only giving you my own opinion.

It seems to me as a fellow member of yours that the most proper course and the most dignified one would have been to ask for the resignation from the Branch of a member who is not agreeable to the others, and surely no one would want to stay among you in such an event. It is true that we should defend one another but it is also true that we should act with discretion and not in such a way as to fasten on our friends charges and aspersions which otherwise would be vague and not referring definitely to any particular person, and further we should be careful to exercise the broadest charity where there is a possible chance — and all the more in the case of a fellow member.

None of the Committee know Mr. X—— personally, and all they have before them is the record showing irregularity that vitiates the whole thing. . . .

After the decision of the committee if against the expulsion the Branch can take up the case again and proceed in a judicious manner even if it be a pursuit of a person who, from your own account, seems to need Charity — on the part of his fellow members. Theosophy demands not only loyalty but also JUSTICE which is the rule of the Masters in Their dealings with us, and we must all admit that if They were as strict with us as we are so often with our fellows we would have been condemned long ago.

I have written to you thus freely because you were so good as to write me on the subject and you will not misjudge the spirit in which I address you.

Fraternally yours,
WILLIAM Q. JUDGE

———

Miss Mary Musaeus,   October 4th 1888.
Washington, D. C.
Dear Madame:

I have your last long letter. It will not be necessary to go so far as to get Mme Blavatsky to "take the seal off Mr. Higgin's lips" about theosophy in Washington because, first, I know all about that which you call "pseudo theosophy" there and the reasons which Mr. Higgins has; and second I did not want to know why you and he did not join the T S there, but only asked if you were members irrespective of the question whether you were in a Branch or unattached to one.

The peculiarities or idiosyncrasies of a single Branch or of its members should not deter us from engaging in the cause of Masters if we believe that They exist. The

T S is meant to be a brotherhood and its members have to learn to bear with, or if you please, have pity for, the foibles and failings of their fellow members, but they have, in the organization, relief from such annoyance as personal contact might cause in that they can go into different Branches or become members at large and continue to work each by his lights for the objects set by the Masters. It is only in this work faithfully and sincerely carried on with no setting of the heart on the reward that the chance may arise of becoming accepted chelas of Masters or of Their advanced chelas.

The Masters of course have many other ways and places for obtaining chelas besides in the T S. They have Their disciples in various parts of India outside of the ranks of the T S, and over a thousand of those have given their sympathy and support to our body, and there are other places where They also have them. But you made your application to the body, formed here in the world by these high beings, and hence in replying to you we have been governed by the rules given us by Them. Chelas or would-be-chelas approaching through the T S have to join the body formed by the Masters and have to work for the furtherance of its objects unselfishly if through that channel they hope to get a fuller realization of what seems desirable to them. Masters have over and over again declared that they do not work for single individuals and will not to them be revealed no matter whether those persons are in the T S or out of it unless the conditions are complied with. Those are in part: a devotion to humanity and a persistence in work to that end and to the end that all the motives shall be purified and also the life. This is why there are many persons of extraordinary attainments who, failing to find the recognition which they think their due, have denied the existence of the Masters — the conditions had not been fulfilled.

I have spoken thus plainly so as to put you in possession of facts that you ought to be aware of and so as to prevent any misunderstanding, and with no other animus whatever. I send you a copy of the proceedings at the last Convention and invite your careful reading of the long letter from Mme Blavatsky therein printed.

Very Truly Yours,

WILLIAM Q. JUDGE.

———

N Y Oct. 5 1888.

Dear Keightley

I have yours enclosing Harte's. Thanks. The dummy is at hand. Shall be glad to get the sheets, but there is so much delay it will not be possible to have the book [*Secret Doctrine*] out by 27th. Will try my best however. The book is splendid from the part found in the dummy. I get a few orders every week.

The prospectus you sent out from London has made bother, since you put the price £1.8 and I at $7.50. But I suppose you have sent out no more. I hope the index is good.

I see she rakes A P S. pretty well. He deserves it as he has stuck on his Esot B — what we call here "mashed"

127

on it – and admits nothing else right. It is easy to see defects in E B even by a casual reader. But he will fade out like a badly developed photograph, and we need not bother.

As to the french racket I could not pronounce on it now. In general the french are no good, and when *one* is found like Gaboriau who will do, do, do, even badly, he ought to be encouraged. And I know that is Masters' idea. The petty rules and jealousies and rights of a lot of members are nothing when they clash with a man who really does for the cause. And so it is in this case. And also with some here in U. S. We have similar troubles, but if an obnoxious man is really working and spreading the ideas I do not much regard the cavils and crying of a lot of people who are good for nothing but to find fault with others.

Masters are guiding an enormous movement and have more concern to have work really carried on – of some, any or all sorts – than to coddle and advance in an abnormal manner any one or more individuals.

And it is also a fact that psychics generally have a few of the common screws loose. They are ½ here and ½ not, and hence they frequently do queer things, but if they do a meritorious work for the Cause they bear the burden of their own faults and do good to the world. I do not excuse their faults, but I do not bother about them. And it is quite plain that a host of grumblers who stick at points of form, right and etiquette while they do no real work for us, are of no account in our summing up. All the better of course it is if the real worker has much tact and virtue, but the conditions do not always combine in our Western world or in any other in this cycle.

So, in this way injustice might be committed. It was a coup de grace to take away the name of Isis but all the same it was error in my judgment even if I did congratulate Olcott. It was just the same about Cooper O who ought to have been put out long ago even if there ensued a holy war.

I do not think H P B has erred at all, and we must not judge by the present and we cannot see the future, but we can wait for it. It is our duty to work and obey without trying to adjust orders with our ideas or those of others or with what are called "rights" of people. So even if you had been rushed over to Paris and back on a fool's chase it is well, provided you were told to do it and proceeded on orders from your nearest superior. Such at least is my judgment. Excuse haste and love to you and the rest
As Ever
WILLIAM Q JUDGE

Personal.   N. Y. Oct 17, 1888
My dear Sir and Brother:

I have yours of 11th in which you say there are enigmas in mine of 2^d which you cannot solve. I did not so intend it. And perhaps the official letter with the decision, now perhaps in your hands will put things in a different light.

I do not see how you can misunderstand the situation. It is this:

(a) You were expelled by the Los A T S.

(b) That makes your expulsion in general from the T. S., until revoked.

(c) It is revoked for irregularity — the only matter the Committee could consider.

(d) Hence, you are now again F. T. S. in good standing.

You say you are a lawyer. That has been my profession for 16 years and is now, and under our T. S. rules an expulsion unrevoked works as such all through the T. S. If they had merely dropped your name from the roll that would have been merely local. If there had been a trial on charges we could consider the *cause;* but as there was not we only could consider the action.

It must be plain to a layman, let alone a lawyer, that they never could convict and expel you on the charge they make. Hence it is plain that they will take no further proceedings and you stand well, for their illegal action is now, under the decision, *no action at all.*

As to the suggestion about resigning it is also plain that as you were illegally expelled and therefore not expelled you are still a member of that Branch. It is not necessary for you to find a meeting of it in order to resign from the local T. S. You can send your resignation by mail to the Secretary of it and you need not bother about what they may do and only need notify me as Gen Sec that you have resigned and are a member at large. Your friend of whom you speak can do the same thing. Resignation is always effective even without acceptance by the body to whom it is addressed.

And it seems to me a wise thing to resign now from the L. A. T. S. and end all official connection with a body in which you are not at home. I cannot forestall anything they may do, but must accord them their rights just as much as I must do the same to you. One of their rights is for them to be able to try you if they are so foolish as to attempt it. I have privately tried to point out to them that such a thing is folly and likely to damage them, since all that you have to do is to remain silent and they can then prove nothing since their asseveration that *they* are the persons referred to would only prove that they had done a similar thing to that spoken of in the article. I hope this is all plain; and recollect it is said to you privately as a fellow member and not as an official.

You err in supposing that from Mrs Ver Planck alone you got help. Another person first suggested to me that I take certain steps in the matter of your expulsion as soon as the Secy notified me. It is true I waited a while. And in other ways you were helped in the silent methods.

Now my dear Brother I know that you are willing to work and I propose to let you, for as you say the laborers are few, and the work sadly needs others; and besides that if there was not this work for you to do *you* might as well be dead. Is it not so? And recollect what Masters say: "We have no personal favorites. We care for the *acts* of people and not for their standing or their mere sentimental aspirations."

I have appreciated all your work and value highly what you have done in the Mystic which will be of greater value when you shall have a T. S. Branch there which will be willing to do all that you say about printing and children and public work comprehensible by the average man. And I shall be glad to assist you in it as I may; and if I could see any way to going to California I would be glad to do that too for a visit in order to help you on the spot as well as the others on the coast. We need work sadly. We are troubled all through the T. S. with barnacles who will do nothing for either themselves or others but stand often in the way of the work that might be done if they were not there. But even for those we must be charitable and must always try to persuade as much as we can, or to steer a middle course, not swerving from our own work as laid down, and at the same time by patience and non resistance prove to others that we can work and let all men do as they please. We must be "allowers of all theologies, compassionaters, perceivers, rapport of men. We reject nothing that is asserted nor the asserters" but we work on, on, ever, to the end that "men may become brothers" as we try to be.

After sending in your resignation as a member of the L. A. T. S. and waiting a reasonable time, proceed with your other plans looking to the establishment of another T. S. You may meet formal opposition from those entitled to notice, but if "you have courage, patience and faith all will be well." And do not talk of resigning from the T. S. or of any such nonsense as letting things go by default. You know that you could not if you tried.

Hoping to hear from you soon,

I am fraternally yours,

WILLIAM Q JUDGE

To Bertram Keightley, Esq 35 Broadway N Y
Oct 26 1888.

My dear Keightley:

Item. I shall start for London in November on the 3d 7th or 10th as I can arrange. The death of my Uncle in Dublin offers an opportunity to go over that I cannot miss. I would have started before this if it had not been for the Secret Doctrine. So you may expect to see me in due course.

The trouble I expected with the Appraiser came on. He sent for me after I had taken out 3 cases, and said that the book [*Secret Doctrine*] was undervalued. On a calculation it appeared that the 1000 copies came to some 30c. each. This of course is too low, and therefore I was stared in the face with the chance of a penalty and double duty. The law is: that we must pay duty here (at 25%) upon the market value of the goods. In this case that is determined by cost of paper and printing; in the case of a book already sold the wholesale price abroad determines the value upon which duty is to be paid.

But after a long argument and great persuasion, and perhaps for other causes, the Appraiser consented to let the book through, with the caution that on the next invoice the true value is to be stated. When I see you I will have the minutest directions regarding 2^d vol.

It is, as I said, impossible to come out on 27. The cases got out of the Cust. H. to the binder on the 23^d only and had to be recollated as American binders will take no risks on your collating and I am only waiting the binding to go away.

133

I will bring over full details of other matters and so will not go into it now, except to observe that no contract has yet been made with a bookseller as agent, since Mr Lovell advised me to have a copy in hand before I went to see about that.

I have selected as colors for cover dark brown and dark blue. I cannot with my limited help attend to all the un-
* work, and so have agreed with the binder that he is to wrap up some 300 copies ready for Fullerton to send out.

My regards to all. Meanwhile I wait in joyful anticipation for a reunion in November.

As Ever
WILLIAM Q JUDGE

* indecipherable

———

Oct. 26th 1888

My dear Bro. Richardson:

If I understand your letter aright, our Boston Brethren are learning through disappointment what might have been earlier learned through examination. If the Theosophical Society had been established as a School of Occultism, or if membership therein had been urged as the step to Occult Powers, or if assurance had been vouchsafed that through the Society would come "radical information on Magic, etc." "in advance of that presented to the world," then truly you and all who have expected, yet have not received, these things would have ground for complaint. But is such the fact? If you read the 3 avowed aims for which the Society was founded, you will see that the 3^d (not the *1st,* by the way) was the *"investigation"* of unexplained laws and of psychical powers, not the *"acquirement"* of such powers. Moreover, in the most explicit terms and on very many occasions, in editorial articles in "Lucifer" and "The Theosophist" and in addresses and letters, the Founders of the T. S. have disavowed any purpose of founding a School of Adeptship or Magic, have never held out any inducement or any hope or even any incitement to a search for "Powers," but have clearly, repeatedly, and urgently explained that the true aim for each individual was spiritual development, that ambition for magical power was as purely selfish and untheosophic as ambition for social or political or any other power, that unselfish consecration to the general good measured the genuine quality of any aspirant, and that supra-natural powers were the collateral attendants upon, not the immediate result of, spiritual illumination.

Now if, in disregard of the avowed aims of the Society and in defiance of the direct teachings and warnings of its highest expositors, any of our Brethren demand an experience different from, and even antagonistic to, that held out, is not disappointment inevitable? And if disappointment is inevitable, is resentment just?

Let us look at the matter from still another view-point. You desire, I understand, magical powers. Why? Because they are curious and pleasing and a nice thing to have; or because you wish to use them to benefit humanity? If

135

the former, there is no more reason for expecting aid towards them from the T. S. than in expecting aid from it towards the acquirement of money or office or any other personal treasure. But if the latter, why should you expect occult powers for benevolent purposes when you do not even use the natural powers on hand? For you talk of leaving the Society, the very agency through which our Revered Heads are working for the expansion of Light and Truth through the world, and which they desire every sincere Theosophist to join as (at present) the most efficient means for assisting Them in Their mission!

I think, my friend, that you could not do greater good to yourself — to say nothing of the Cause — than by revising your conception of Theosophy, and the Theosophic mission, and the motive best for each Theosophist. If the result of this should be a conviction that the surest path to Light and Strength is over the prostrate forms of all mere personal desires, and that the more one works for others the more he ultimately gains for himself — in fact, though not from intention, you will partake of the spirit of Damodar, and so may hope for his success. And if the other members of the Boston T. S. come to like conclusions, we shall no more hear of constant dissension and possible dissolution, but of united effort in the spread of Theosophic truth and of self-forgetful interest in every good word and work.

Always faithfully and fraternally yours,
WILLIAM Q. JUDGE

1889

C. H. Whitaker Esq   Jan 11 1889
Dear Sir
    I cannot throw light on the matter of the glossary.
Perhaps it was found to be too great a work and too much
for the expense. I think it will be gotten out. But really
one of those Eastern books sold by Scribner with the words
in them ought to be owned by us all, and personally I
think it was too much to offer a glossary with the Secret
Doctrine. A *real* Glossary would involve 3 vols more.
                         Sincerely
                     WILLIAM Q JUDGE

Dr. C. W. Bush,   Jan. 30, 1889
    Pres. Los Angeles T S
Dear Sir and Bro:
    I beg to inform you that the Executive committee met
on the 28th inst and considered the matter of the application for a Branch in Los Angeles to be called Sattwa, and
after reading the objections and correspondence have come
to the conclusion that no valid reason has been given for
a refusal to issue the charter which has been regularly
applied for by over five members.
    The Committee thinks that all members should try to
bury dissensions and that whenever in a town a split or
disagreement occurs in a Branch it is much better to per-

mit one party to form another Branch, if they should so desire — and there is no insuperable objection — for in that way the work may be carried on in many different directions. They are very sorry that any trouble has occurred, and they direct me to say that they think it much wiser to let all the personalities in this matter come to an end, whatever may have been the supposed offense of any person, and it seems to them that if the matter was pressed very much farther it would become more disagreeable at every step, and would never tend to the adjustment of the difficulties or peace.

As I am informed, the new Branch has no intention or desire to interfere with your work and there seems to be plenty of room in your city for more than two Branches.

The newspaper report which was sent here was not thought by the Committee to have weight, because such reports have been constantly made and such charges reiterated about the Society, its leaders and the Adepts for the last 14 years, in all parts of this country, Asia and Europe, and I have always found that whenever any one starts the subject of theosophy before the public, a storm of ridicule is evoked; and I beg to tell you that one of the instructions sent by one of the Adepts, in writing, is, that the Society and its work must be spread before the world as much as possible. This applies to the exoteric and not to the esoteric work.

Your Branch still has the right to appeal to the Convention in April.

Fraternally Yours
WILLIAM Q JUDGE
General Secretary

Dear Bro. Dick   Feb. 3 1889

I got yours of 21 Jan and am obliged. But I cannot
hope to reply as I am too busy. May I ask you to send
me each month some little note of the work and affairs in
Dublin and I will use it in Path, as I shall your present
letter. Will try and send you a photo as you ask — perhaps
in this letter.

Glad you saw H P B. The visit did you good. I hope
the work will go on further and it seems to be growing a
little in Old Dublin. If we work the Masters always help.
They need instruments and cannot effect good ends where
all is apathy: hence the value of *any* work with a sincere
heart.

My love to all in Dublin and believe me ever your
brother   WILLIAM Q JUDGE

———

Dear Arch   5 Feby 1889

So awfully busy. No time to write. Got yours. Sent
you the supplies. They had gone when yours came saying
they were for 32 Rem. Mach. Glad your room is fixed up,
and hope you will sell the novels and salt the few rupees
resulting into your pocket.

There will be endless delays about S. Sec. but let them
wait and think, it will do them good. If they cant get on
without instructions they cant with them.

Hope you understand that your idea to send all direct
from London is in accord with mine.

141

How would you like to exchange with Fullerton. You to come here and work with me and he to go there to London? He is good at system and away from *my* chilling sphere he gets on first rate: as he never will understand me. I am in earnest and bespeak your prayerful thought on the subject. Ask H P B how it would fit. He would keep all the books etc etc with great regularity and attend to all matters and do literary work of great value to the T S., T P S., and all the rest.

Meanwhile I am rushed. Am getting out a record edition of Patanjali in your english and think it will sell. It will go to the printer a week or two.

As Ever old man

WILLIAM Q

———

Mrs. Alice M Wyman   Feb. 8, 1889.
Dear Madam:

The experiences you relate are those common in mediumship. You cannot help the girl to anything but mediumship and that is a detriment. Already she has attracted to her the worst of elementaries — a suicide — and no one can tell when others may get in the same road. All the teaching I know is against mediumship but not against cultivating an acquaintance with ones own spirit — this is never done by mediumship.

Better bring such things to a close, and try to surround the girl and yourself with thoughts of spirit and not of matter — for these experiences are all of matter. The girl is all mixed up even in her psychic flights with monks and priests and so on, and you cannot tell when a messenger of Master may speak through her (and that is not probable) and when not. A Guru does not come by mediumship but silently reveals within and in dreamless sleep. The right road is indicated in the Memo. and rules.

The first instruction will soon be forwarded from London. Meanwhile patience is a virtue.

Sincerely yours,
WILLIAM Q. JUDGE.

Mrs. A. M. Wyman   Feb. 13, 1889.
Dear Madam:

I have yours and am glad to read its contents.

The clairaudience and clairvoyance you refer to is not the function of the spirit but is the work altogether and in every case of the merely psychic senses, and have nothing to do with the spirit.

The latter can only be reached when we have become master of the body and of all sense.

The advice you got was good about the books and was no doubt a message given to the spooks by your own higher self or that of the other person. But in these matters one must accept only that which one is sure is from the higher self.

Fraternally yours,
WILLIAM Q. JUDGE

My dear Arch: Feb 17 1889.

I have yours with enclosure. Yes, I am sorry you are not on the exchange list. I havent got any one yet, but hope in god.

Now as you say these "Revised Rules" of Hartes are nothing less than damnable. They are wrong, silly and hugely full of elements for trouble and dismay. His dismay will begin when he gets my letter of today, for I plainly tell him that we wont have it and will tear his constitution into bits first. It is the product of his brain. It begins nowhere and ends at no place. Just read the objects p.p. 53 and 54. He has cut off end of 2d and the words he has cut off embody the last 14 years efforts of H P B's life. And then 3d object he has made an abortion of by his injecting "pursued by a portion of the fellows" and the next sentence in brackets is put, unauthorized, and 2d, a lie, for the E. S. T. S. has nothing to do with Rules of T. S. or objects. And "Secy in Partibus"! What silly imitation of R. C. "in partibus infidelium." I have laid him out in 8 p.p. and ended by saying he might crawl through a hole and telegraph me "limited" meaning that the voluntary system is limited to India. Next week I am sending out to every Branch a notice to same effect, and at Convention I shall sit on it as hard as I know how. Such is my mind; and I feel very tired. He will do something else that will be a killer or else he will be sat on. The trouble is he has no one there to sit on him and will be quite unrestrained. He has a passion for machinery

144

of a great size and these Revised Rules are his first chance since I sat on his "Elder Brother" scheme in 1886.

Well I havent time for more as you can imagine what a wealth of work has dropped on me since Alexander left — and it is likely to increase. Am hoping to have somebody fly in the window soon.

Will move Path office to 21 Park Row in March and then will have larger spaces not palatial but good and in a fine building where the elevator (lift!) does not run slow nor stop at 5.

Please note inclosed proof of my new American edition of Patanjali edited by me and dedicated to H P B. Am selling it already. Price $1.25. Better notice and advertise it.

Adieu then. Love to the brethren — Please tell H P B to surely send me a letter to read to convention and to also send me a rescript that this fee business is limited to India.

As Ever

William Q

———

Dr J. F. Miller, Esq.,   Feb. 20th 1889.
Dear Sir and Brother: —

Your favor in regard to your patient was duly received but owing to pressure of work, and also owing to the letter and enclosures being slightly illegible I have not given them quite the attention I otherwise would, and therefore will write to you on the basis of that which you said to me last night.

145

The case is not an unusual one. Through the unfortunate subject having allowed her thoughts to dwell too much on the man she loves, and he having allowed his to dwell too much on her, and these thoughts evidently not having always been of the purest there has been an elemental developed which taking the shape of her lover has fixed itself upon her as an incubus. Such cases are, sad as it is to have to admit it, not of phenomenally rare occurrence. No exorcism, and no remedies can be efficacious excepting insofar as they — the remedies — to a certain extent may * your patient from the effort to control her body, and allow her to thus give greater attention to regaining the mastery over herself. The regaining of this mastery is, of course, a slow process. She must interest herself in lines of thought, particularly thought connected with action, which will so engross her mind that the thought of her lover gradually vanishes therefrom. Nature abhors a vacuum, and like air rushing into empty spaces the old thoughts will, when her mind is not filled with others rush in to fill the void space and with them will rush in this elemental power which she has developed. She has gone down hill; she must now climb up the hill, even if with pain and difficulty. She and her lover little by little, imperceptibly and gradually have allowed themselves to fall from the highest plane of regard to a lower one of lust. He is not all to blame. She must have done her part; and when she has again done her part and retrieved the past she will be free from the baneful presence, and, whether her lover will or not, it must seek gratifica-

* indecipherable

146

tion elsewhere. Perhaps you think I have talked more common sense than theosophy, but you must not forget that in one sense theosophy *is* common sense par excellence; and he who looks only for doctrine, or some new or strange thing will be generally disappointed. And now one word in parting; all those external helps which you as a faithful physician will suggest are of the utmost importance. I refer to the use of a moderate and bland diet; the avoidance of stimulants, even tea and coffee, care especially in having the last meal a light one and not taken too soon before retiring, and the having the sleeping room well ventilated, the avoidance of heavy bed clothes, and an abundance of out-door daily exercise, etc. Although the external is but a manifestation or clothing of the internal yet the external itself powerfully affects the internal, and when a severe and doubtful internal struggle is going on a little carelessness about the external may decide for defeat rather than victory. Trusting that I may have served you I am

Yours fraternally
WILLIAM Q JUDGE

Mrs D L Sherburne   Feb 22 1889
   Los Angeles Calif
Dear Madame:

Replying to your letter, I would advise you to join the T. S. Branch.

The spirit of the Branch should not be that it needs a teacher and cannot get on without one. The T. S. is a

Brotherhood and each unit (Branch) as well as each unit therein (member) should do all that they can for the Cause. When the disciples are ready the teachers will appear. By doing just what it can in studying theosophical doctrines, and *with their own minds* the members of a Branch will grow and teach each other, for as yet it is not teachers that are wanted, but the preparation found in study, work and self-discipline. The Branch should also try to spread before the people — without proselyting — the doctrines of Theosophy such as Brotherhood, Karma and Reincarnation, and meanwhile should exemplify Brotherhood, and act with energy as well as discrimination.

The first steps in true occultism are Self discipline, self knowledge and devotion to the interests of others — i.e.: unselfishness. One cannot hope to be a chela until the elementary steps are gone through. Your own heart will tell you how much you are prepared for chelaship. Secondly, the adepts when they do take a chela nearly always stop psychic powers for a while, until the disciple has got to know himself, his faults, his follies, his vices and his thoughts as well as his virtues.

By attentively reading the Path you will find much that you seek. See for instance in Feb. Path p. 342.

I enclose applications.

Fraternally yours
WILLIAM Q JUDGE

P. O. Box 2659, N. Y. City
Feby, 22. 1889.

My dear Griscom;

Your sketch of a plan for the working of branches of the T. S. came duly to hand. Please accept my thanks for the same. Now will you add a little more to the obligation by doing a little more thinking for me. I have in mind publishing in the "Path" from time to time subjects for discussion at the meetings of the branches, the discussion of these subjects being entirely voluntary, but done so nearly as possible in the same week by those which accept the suggestions. The harvest is so full that it grieves me constantly that the workers are not more ready. That there are workers waiting, and many of them too, I know, but they do not seem to know how to begin work. A little infusion of courage, of zeal, of faith and of confidence is all that is needed. I consider myself happy in doing the little which I can. But that which I can do is not only little, but others fail to receive the benefits which would accrue to them by doing on their own parts. Our members must not forget that they must rise by action, and by long, hard, steady action, to a higher state. It will not do for them to lie like hungry birds in the nest waiting with open bills for the mother to bring them food. They must out and search for their own food. They must be up and doing. No matter how crude their efforts they must make them. The beginning is always hard, but the sooner it is made the better. And I see no better way for them to make the beginning, after the regular duties of life are performed, than by activity in the cause. Right

149

thought is one of the greatest of gifts, so let those that have it give it to their fellow seekers. And let them too get from their fellow seekers, so that they may as time passes be more and more, and being more and more have more and more to give. But to get down again to the point of departure, I like your suggestions. I want more and fuller ones; and also, as I said, a list of subjects suitable for discussion, and with it if possible, a brief analysis of each and also the names of books bearing upon it, so that members having the subject presented to them long before the time of meeting and being told where to look for information can be so prepared as to have each one something of interest for others. Those who have not the gift of speaking can at least read a quotation or two.

Will you undertake to overthrow my undertaking to furnish lists of subjects for discussion in the branches, and I will print them in the "Path"?

It is not necessary to go over all the possible subjects at once, but to show the manner in which the various doctrines may be discussed and applied in all directions. For example: KARMA. What is Karma? How many kinds of Karma are there, Is there left-over Karma? Do we exhaust in this life all previous Karma? (No) What sort of Karma is made by kicking an orange peel off the sidewalk? (This is called a sort of weak but still good Karma) etc. etc.

Waiting your answer I am,

Sincerely yours,

WILLIAM Q JUDGE

P. O. Box 2659
N. Y. Mar. 24 1889

My dear Brother Dick:

I have yours and have also received the Dublin T. S. Journal. Give my thanks please for the latter. Your letter is interesting, and I would like to hear once a month from Dublin Lodge so as to insert the item in the Path. A little item could be made up for me each month and posted to me. You can see by the Path what way it should be made up. I have great difficulty in getting these items, and trust my countrymen will respond. Just drop the item in the mail and dont bother about formal letters unless you have time. If you send the item on the 10th I will get it on 20th. If later then it is too late.

Am very glad there is activity in Dublin. There always will be activity if members are not afraid, but make it known and follow the words of the Master to me, "let the society prosper on its moral worth." That is, teach and promulgate our ethics. They will take hold everywhere, and by giving all people the chance to see the light, you will gain the adhesion of those who are waiting for theosophy, and there are many of those.

The world needs the cure found in our philosophy and ethics, and mystery and esotericism can be left for those to find who are really capable. The majority of men are not fit for the occult, but they are all fit and ready for true ethics and right form of thought.

I have great hopes for Dublin Lodge. I think that paper in Theosophist was from your Lodge, and it is a good paper — much higher and deeper than the sapient

151

commentator who saw fit to add an inadequate note to it.

Our Adyar T. S. proposes some new "transactions," and when they are out we will send over some to dear tea drinking and car driving Dublin.

Present my affectionate regards to all, and believe me, as ever yours

WILLIAM Q JUDGE

Private   May 17 1889
R Wes McBride Esq
My Dear Bro:

With the American gentleman to whom you refer there is nothing now the matter but merely a heavy and perhaps for him dangerous outbreak of egotism and spite. The latter is due to his failure to rule or ruin the T. S. in U. S. for although our Rules permit of no president he has become embittered because we did not all rush to his feet and elect him such. This he has written H P B (I have seen the letter) and she has replied "do theosophical work and hinder not that of others and I'll support you." With him however it is "aut Caesar aut nihil" as by bitter experience I know. As to the other person nothing need surprise. Her letter is a self accusation. The *truth* is that an Adept named only to a few did actually dictate Light on Path. Throw a mantle of charity over this failure and watch yourself. Light on Path still remains a gem.

Sincerely

WILLIAM Q JUDGE.

21 Park Row,
New York, U. S. May 22, 1889

Rt. Rev. H. H. Sumangala,
Colombo, Ceylon.

Respected sir:

Pardon me, a stranger, for addressing you without introduction, but I trust that I can offer you a sufficient excuse. Permit me therefore to state briefly that I am the Vice-President of the Theosophical Society; the General Secretary of the Society in the United States of America, the President of the New York branch of the Society; and that I was taken into the Church [Buddhist] over which you preside by Col. H. S. Olcott in 1884, at which time I was in India.

My object in addressing these lines to you is, to say that, in my opinion, there now exists in this country an opportunity for the extension of Buddhism, provided that competent men of your country could in some way be obtained to work to that end here. There are nearly 50,000,000 of people in this country, who for many years have been living under a free form of government, who have all been more or less educated, and who all constantly read the thousands of newspapers and magazines which are published here every day. As a result of this freedom of action and of thought they have, to a great extent, come to the conclusion that Sectarian Christianity is more or less of a failure, and especially as they all see its professors failing to follow the law of the supposed founder of the church.

153

In consequence of the steady efforts made by the Theosophical Society during the last fourteen years, the people have had their attention directed to Theosophical doctrines and to Eastern religions and philosophies, and while it is true that a great number do not know what "Theosophy" means, the greater number of the people know something about Buddhism. I should also say that even Sectarian religious papers here have lately and frequently said, with alarm, that no doubt many people here would flock to hear Buddhism preached. I know that the people of this country are quite ready to understand and be benefitted by a proper exposition of the doctrine of the Buddhist church.

But if Buddhism is preached here solely by an American or European there will be a great disposition to criticise and perhaps laugh at him on the ground that he being a European or American cannot know what Buddhism is, since so many learned Europeans dispute as to its real meaning.

I have therefore for some time thought that if a Buddhist priest, or more than one, were to come here and work with the people, churches could be founded and the doctrine disseminated very widely and rapidly; and I thought that perhaps you might be able better than any one I know of to either find such willing persons or to designate them for the work.

I cannot now however offer any livelihood or money to carry on such work, but if I had a favorable reply from you I might be able to make arrangements in respect to the living here of such a person. And if such an one were to be sent here he would have to be a tried and proved man, because he would be subjugated to various temptations, such as flattery, adulation, attempts to draw him into a faction, or to convert him to some other method or belief. I speak from experience in respect to this for I have seen such things occur here with men who came from eastern lands.

I beg therefore that you will take this matter into consideration and that you will favor me with a reply, for I have this matter very much at heart, and in consequence of a very wide acquaintance with the religious thought of the people here, I am satisfied that true Buddhism preached by a Buddhist priest properly authorized by you, would secure many believers.

Permit me to subscribe myself, with great respect,

Sincerely yours,

WILLIAM Q. JUDGE

———

Mr. Peter Long,   June 4, 1889

St. Paul, Minn.

Dear Sir and Brother:

The charges of fraud against Madame Blavatsky have been often made and as often refuted. The last, the one to which you refer, is of the peculiarly outrageous and virulent type. In conjunction with Dr. Keightley of London, an intimate friend and member of the household of

Madame Blavatsky, I have prepared a conclusive answer to this charge, which went to the printer this morning and will be sent to every F. T. S. in a few days. This will give you more information than I can at present write out.

If you will read the "Occult World," "Incidents in the Life of Madame Blavatsky," and the last chapter of the "Wilkesbarre Letters" you will see much about the character and life of our Honored Head. Further, if you wish to see the demolition of Mr. Hodgson's "Exposure" of Madame Blavatsky, you can read the pamphlets entitled the "Occult World Phenomena" by Mr. Sinnett, and the pamphlet by Dr. Hartmann in which are given the affidavits and other testimony of the witnesses who were present at the very phenomena which Mr. Hodgson attempted to deny. Mr. Hodgson's pamphlet was a report to the Society for psychical research.

There is to me something peculiarly incongruous in the idea that a person who is really a trickster and a fraud should, nevertheless, sacrifice health, property, and almost life in an effort to promote a system of the purest morals and the highest spirituality. Tricks are resorted to for personal advantage or profit in some form; but in Madame Blavatsky's case all personal advantage has been disregarded from the very first, and her life has been one of constant hardship and self-sacrifice. Of course self-sacrifice does not prove the truth of doctrine, but it certainly shows the sincerity of the person practicing it.

I have myself known Madame Blavatsky most intimately for 14 years, and my opinion of her disinterestedness and integrity was never more than it is now and I know her to be all and more than is claimed by her best friends.

Very truly and fraternally yours,

WILLIAM Q. JUDGE

Dr. Coues is a Theosophist who seeks personal aggrandisement and failing in that tries to damage those who would not let him seize the T. S. to use it for his own vanity.

Hodgson's "exposé" is only to be had from the Psychical Res. Soc. of London.

Gen. R P Hallgreen.   June 12th 1889

Dear Sir and Brother,

In reply to your letter: I think if you will examine your papers that you will find that members of E S are not asked to protest *as such*. As members E S and therefore presumably having the honor and defence of the whole Society and its leaders at heart more than others, they are asked to protest against such things *as come under their notice.* They are not asked to buy all papers and *search* for attacks, but to protest against such when found.

No person is to be kept in the dark. All have right to just so much Wisdom as they are fitted to receive or such power as they are fitted to exercise. Reflect that astral powers are a very serious responsibility as a possession and the Wisdom in their use cannot be appreciated much less acquired by all indiscriminately.

The Wisdom and the powers connected with it will be acquired by you and all men as they fit themselves for it

157

and as they can *make* their rightful demand felt by * to give. Mme Blavatsky is doing a great work for the world and she gives to E. S. knowledge which she alone possesses. At least she is the only possessor of the knowledge to whom all men alike can obtain ready access. Therefore she demands that those who wish to be her pupils shall help her in the work she is doing for Humanity and shall themselves practise the axioms and work for the Theosophical Society.

I thank you for your rec. of the "Instructions."

We have an American Edition of Patanjali which contains the Indian Edition $1.00 of which I enclose you prospectus. We will forward it on receipt of reply. The Indian Ed cannot be had.

Yrs fraternally,

WILLIAM Q JUDGE

* indecipherable

Mr. Jakob Bonggren,   June 13, 1889
   Chicago, Ill.
Dear Sir and Brother:

Many thanks for your circular. . . .

I congratulate you on your correct understanding of the pledge with regard to the documents. As there is to be a re-organization of the E. S. I trust that all black sheep will be speedily got rid of and left to their karma, for which I sincerely pity them.

Yours fraternally

WILLIAM Q JUDGE

My Dear Mr. Higgins:

I send you the Charter herewith, and was obliged to put in the names in the order in which they appeared in the application. I do this early this morning so that you may get it and hence cannot say much, but I do want to say that thinking over last night what you said about Somner and Co, there is "another" that fights for us and I do not think that you need bother your mind in any respect about it. Indeed my experience in this is (as distinguished from other matters) that when plans are laid in any way with respect to the motives of others we are likely to fail. And I know also that while the opposition you speak of may be made it will affect nothing. All the mistakes made by them will be for our benefit provided we act without interest in results. I will send the books soon.

Sincerely yours,

WILLIAM Q JUDGE

————

June 21, 1889

To the Editor of The Journal, Chicago, Ill.
Dear Sir:

Will you give place for a small act of justice?

In your issue of June 15th the Rev. David Swing has an article entitled "A New Gypsy Queen," in which he says that Madame Blavatsky receives gold from the chelas as they sweep by. This is no doubt a fine piece of sarcasm, but as it is utterly false it does a great injustice to Madame Blavatsky, whose friend and lawyer I have been for 15 years past. As such permit me to say that her property is as follows, and no more: an interest in the "Theosophist" which does not pay; an interest in the magazine "Lucifer" which is in debt; a copyright of the book "Isis Unveiled" which in 11 years has paid her about $300; a copyright of the "Secret Doctrine" which has not yet paid.

As General Secretary of the Society above named referred to in Mr. Swing's article, allow me to say that Madame Blavatsky receives no part of any of the fees of such Society, and that such fees are the large sum of $1 a year from each member.

Will you permit me to ask whether the Rev. gentleman, David Swing, receives a salary?

Yours truly

WILLIAM Q. JUDGE

———

My Dear Olcott: July 6, 1889.

I wish to inform you of an important matter in confidence for the present and so that you may be advised.

As lately the enemies of the T S here in the persons of Coues and Bundy of the R P J [Religio-Philosophical Journal] have become very virulent and determined to hurt and impede us in every way and by any means, and as I found out that Coues had the idea of incorporating under our name and thus scooping us and afterwards enjoining us, I made up my mind that it was time to get ahead of him, so I have incorporated a Society under the the name of the THEOSOPHICAL SOCIETY AND UNIVERSAL BROTHERHOOD under our state laws, and have had the same done as far as possible by our best members in the other states. We shall present the charters to the next convention and thus protect the society from those who wish to do it harm.

This does not mean that the T. S. is incorporated for it will take time to get all the Branches in under this; but it is only a matter of time and letter writing. I do not think it is well to make mention of this yet until we have all fixed. Of course at the convention we will as usual declare and continue our allegiance to the headquarters.

Can't you put a stopper on Harte. He is running wild and using the magazine to announce and enforce his private views and they by no means are those of the majority. You had better look out also for his over zeal or he will get the T S in India into a box meddling with things not in its purview. It is in his mind, and although I like him I also know him and know that you must keep him down to good well defined editing and not let him run off with the machine. I have written to him until I am sick but can get nothing out of him. His change of rules was a fad that we sat on here years ago and he knew that this section emphatically was opposed to such changes. And that he has not yet explained and I have asked him to many a time. I am in dead earnest, and am quite willing that he should know all that I say; I know him to be the most *un* practical man that ever lived and one who should keep his hand out of the administration pie. Just read the June Theosophist and tell me what you think of the first article. Are we to have a Rome at Adyar, and what is he driving at unless he means to turn the society into some outside reform, and thus cripple it?

As ever yours,

WILLIAM Q JUDGE

Sep 3, 1889

My dear Pryse:

I have your letter, and fully appreciate your feelings as they resemble my own.

I do not think your position is so strange or remarkable as to be beyond our ken, nor do I look at your experiences as being solely mediumistic, nor at the dream or vision as unsolvable. You are now struggling with the *personal self* in the early stages, and can consider yourself fortunate that you have the chance to overcome in the initial battle.

1. You have a natural tendency — as everyone — to accentuate your own experience. Pray consider it first of all as *worthless,* and then you will be in position to understand it and not before.

2. Your vision that when you looked at H P B and saw no old woman but a *God* is correct. You were privileged to see the Truth — For the Being in that old body called H P Blavatsky is a mighty Adept working on his own plan in the world. And thus we do not need to go to Tibet or

S. America to find the sort of Being so many wish to see. Yet having seen the reality better keep silent and work with that in view. For even did you go and tell Him you knew He was there he would smile while he waited for you to do something such as you could in your limited sphere. For flattery counts not and professions are worse than useless. But it is a great thing to *see* as much as you have, and a greater thing it will be if you do not doubt — for you may never see *it* again.

3. The other, about the Tree etc was a vision — or dream — given you to show you the Path. The old tree is H P B and the short cut lies through her. And it will remain open only 10 years or so. The upset and the cane and all that mean that you may be or are upset as is natural. What then are you to do? Just wait first, and second, try to get the calmness — of despair if need be — of certainty, hope and faith if possible.

You are making too much fuss with yourself. Call this all natural and having drawn the lesson, say that it dont amount to much, that you are not a great seer nor saint nor villain, but that you *will* strive to the light and to do some work such as fate shall permit, in the Cause of that Being. Altruism does not refer only to money. It refers to everything.

I will confer with you so that we may see if you are on firmer ground and if there can be anything done or planned.

Meanwhile I am

As Ever yours

WILLIAM Q JUDGE.

P. O. Box 2659.   21 Park Row,
New York, Sep 9 1889.

Dear Bro Dick

Yours of 27 Aug. recd. Am in an awful hurry and so
must be brief.

Lane was an awful liar and *all* he says or said about
me is a lie. There is really nothing to puzzle if we keep
our minds off of persons and their acts. But as to H P B
you cannot judge her by any rule. There is a great Adept
there and he uses that body for His own purposes, both
for use and for trial of others.

Am glad you stand right and hope you always will.
All is well here and in a rush.

Sincerely
WILLIAM Q JUDGE.

———

Private and not for publication.

E. I. K. Noyes, Esq.   N. Y. Oct 11, 1889

Dear Sir and Bro:

I beg to acknowledge yours enclosing copy of letter
sent by you to Col. H. S. Olcott, for which latter accept
my thanks. Yours to me was unsigned.

It seems useless to argue all the matters set forth in
your two favors, or to tell you my own position, since you
have started out with absolute misrepresentations of my
attitude and ideas and conduct and with imaginary straw
obstacles which you wish to demolish.

164

The only thing in yours with which I fully agree and have always asserted, as you can find in print if you care to look, is that there should be and shall be no popery and no hero worship in the T. S. That is well known — except perhaps to you — to be my position.

Our great Theosophical desideratum is justice, another is truth, and another is accuracy. Justice to the T. S., to you and to me would have required you to find out upon what charges and by whom Dr. Coues was expelled; truth would have demanded that the facts be stated, and accuracy would have prevented your mixed up together matters that had no relation to each other.

Mme Blavatsky's name was not mentioned in the expulsion of Dr. Coues as a cause therefor. He was *not* expelled for expressing his opinion about her, and the entire Ex. Com^t· voted upon the charges. His expulsion was the culmination of some years of his efforts to hurt the T. S. and its members. The Gnostic's charter was revoked because it paid no dues, made no reports and had no actual existence, being without any officers and holding no meetings.

It is untrue, as you impute, that I have publicly said that the T. S. *is* H. P. B.; or that I have publicly said she was "as I thought an Adept." My private opinion as to what or who she is has nothing to do with this matter, nor is it a concern of yours, and you didn't act fairly in stating what you did about that in yours to Col. Olcott.

Do not imagine that I have any quarrel with you. Far from it. I desire simply to lay facts before you about which you did not become informed before acting, and to state that you seem to wish to place me in an attitude I never assumed and never would and have always written against. Hence I ask if you think you have acted fairly and in a brotherly spirit to me.

Yours fraternally,

WILLIAM Q JUDGE

———

Oct. 16 1889

Dear Dick

Your long letter at hand, and have made a good item of it for Path. Give me good a/c of H S O's pilgrimage and I'll print it. Long Ireland may live! and Bully for Allan! Give him my best fraternal and all other regards. Wish I were with you to see the fun as there is enough dirt here in the U. S. to make a man sick. Glad B. K. is to go too, as he needs it and he's a splendid fellow: of such there be few. Send along one of your booklets. Have started a small press here with an F T S in charge and shall print lots and save expense.

If you dont give me a/c of H S O I'll never get it. Lane has petered out. He was very bad, but he's trying all over the U S to hurt us. It's a big territory 4000 miles across and it'll take him a good while.

Love to all. As ever

WILLIAM Q JUDGE

Dear Throckmorton:

Yours just at hand. You are right about the scale. All depends upon that, but we cannot yet find out the various scales since we are not prepared for it. The sound is basic and is used in every nation. The Masons have it and speak of it in the 28° of the Scottish Rite, but of course know really nothing of it. They even go so far as to call it a substitute.

In writing it is not possible to properly explain it. But as the key of "f" is the Key of Nature, that is the one to use. However at first the key is hardly important because but few if any get any key right and our keys are on the piano which is false.

I explained fully to Page, but as there is always a good deal of diffidence in anyone when trying this before others he probably was affected by that. But the first sound is a sort of mournful Ah, the 2d is ōō and the 3 must be pronounced smoothly together. This is a matter of practise.

There is the greatest difference between the effect of its pronunciation aloud and any mental use of it. The other words are intended to carry off the vibration of Aum when reached so that they shall go all over the bodily frame.

This is about as well as I can do in a letter. The caution given in the Instructions about not using it in anger or folly should be observed, for there are forces at work in the E. S. that its members do not see or understand.

Sincerely yours,

WILLIAM Q. JUDGE

Please read this to Page and Kerr.

New York Oct 26 1889

Dear Throckmorton

1. Lane is out of **E S** but has not been yet expelled from T. S. He can stay as far as I am concerned. Unwittingly he will cause good. The open letter seems to me to be clearly *only* in reference to the E. S.

2. Much obliged for the diagram. It is interesting and so is the addendum.

3. As to the word and its pronunciation. There is *no* inbreathing. Inbreathing means death. It is all outbreathing. It begins Ah mournfully and the next is run into it. The thrill is a symptom of its being done right. There should also be as it were another oversound as from another sphere a person produced. The varieties of its pronunciation are infinite as the musical scale. And of course *we* have not got *the* right absolutely right sound, for that would blow up St Louis.

If properly done it will do good physically and mentally. Never should it be done in anger nor with evil thoughts.

Read this letter from 3 to your group and also, please write Mrs Slater and ask her to meet you and Mr Page same day so that you can give her the word and its sound for her use. She is in correspondence group.

Fraternally
WILLIAM Q JUDGE
Sec to H P B .·.

Mr. Samuel H. Clapp,   October 29, 1889
17 Lansdowne Road, Holland Park, London W, England
My dear Sam: —

Was glad to get your letter and Alec was very much pleased to hear about you. I need hardly say that I hope you will make a straight hit there and keep matters concerning yourself as they ought to be, for otherwise American stock will not only remain below par but will cease to have any value and furthermore will be considered as distinctly dangerous. There is fun over there no doubt. About your resignation you can fix it any way you like, either remaining as a member-at-large or the Aryan. Which do you wish? I am as usually very busy. In fact so busy that neither Alec nor I know whether we are the work or the workers. For God sake try and make the London people do up their packages for this Country in some manner that is respectable and with stiff paper. I will let the Countess know later on about the T. P. S. pamphlets.

Sincerely as ever,

WILLIAM Q JUDGE

Dear Griffiths: Nov. 23, 1889.

Very glad to hear from you and to receive the report of the Convention. It appears to be the fact that all those who earnestly work are men and women who have to work hard for their living. I am like you, and have:

169

(1) the Path (2) the T. S. (3) the N. Y. T. S. (4) My law business (5) the E. S. etc etc. It is ceaseless. . . .

Now as to E. S. Important. 1st H. P. B. says that U. S. Lodges shall be numbered but they may use a name among themselves.

2d The number must not be given out.

3d The *place of meeting* must not be divulged outside of the group nor its number. This is a definite and absolute rule that must be followed.

I have known of this rule a good many years. H. P. B. has mentioned two or three lodges to me such as Luxor etc but has never divulged the *place* of meeting neither to me nor to Olcott. Please therefore inform all the groups in your Section. If it has been unintentionally broken in the past it must be sacredly kept in the future. This is about all the strict rules of the kind just now.

The "Voice" is out. It is splendid, and shows what true occultism demands.

Sincerely yours
WILLIAM Q JUDGE

—— 1890 ——

My dear Countess: N. Y. Feb. 25 1890

This photographic affair will drive us both crazy unless we end it, and I propose to do that.

I propose to now settle all questions respecting the photos of Masters by paying for those I have at the rates you ask, although I think them high and that you have been swindled by the photographers.

(1) I received of the large H. P. B. reproductions — life size — only two, one in brown, and one grey. Of these I sold one at $7.00 (no matter what Mr. Fullerton may have understood) as I could not get $10. for it and I kept the other to use in headquarters here. Hence I owe you for those, which at your own rates of $10 is — $20.

(2) I have two small photos of the Masters and two large ones, four in all. The two large ones I have given a friend to keep and as I do not know the price I must leave it to you to inform me. The two small ones I have in hand as trustee and shall return them if you please as I shall not be a party to selling pictures of the Masters. Hence you will please add to the $20. for H. P. B.'s the price of the two large photos of Masters and draw against me upon the T. P. Co, that is, let the T. P. Co. pay you and charge it in the a/c agst me that I have with them. Let me know at once the total amount.

This therefore brings this business to a conclusion. I have given orders in the Path office not to order any photos

173

of anyone and not to receive any, but to send them back, and to refer all persons direct to London. As to the photos of Masters I consider the whole thing a scandal. In one breath they are sacred and then they are sold for money. It does not excuse to say that they cost that, for if they are to go to *certain proper* persons then they should be free and if that can't be afforded then they should not be at all. Of course I do not criticize you in any way for I have no right and I do not think you originated it; but I am only expressing my private opinion as I think I can safely do with you as with no one else.

Hoping to hear from you soon

I am sincerely yours

WILLIAM Q JUDGE

Chas. O. Pierson, Esq.   Mar 3, 1890
    Pres^t of B. T. S.
Dear Sir and Bro:

Your important letter at hand. 1st As to B. T. S.* Karma; it has its Karma but I do not think it bad, what bad Karma there is belongs as yet to *individuals* and not to B. T. S.

2^d I note what you say about the B. T. S. and other Branches, etc. Now I want to bring to your personal and *judicial* notice as an F. T. S. and a philosopher, that the very attitude you state as yours is *what has* hurt the B. T. S.

*[Blavatsky T.S. Branch of Washington, D. C.]

174

hitherto. That is an attitude which in effect means that only the B. T. S. may exist there. You have not yet put it thus but it will come to that. Now the true rule and the one given to me in writing from those behind the T. S. is the same for Branches as for persons; they must try and do their duty not regarding the praise, the blame or the assistance of others, and if they take an opposing attitude they arouse force against themselves. All wrong effort will die, all right effort will live — and a week or 6 months will not decide that question. You may not know, but, when the B. T. S. was started there were others in D. C. who wanted another Branch and have always spoken of it. But your late Pres't bitterly opposed it against my advice, and in consequence a strong current of opposition was aroused and still exists. You surely do not wish to add to this; and out of my 15 years' experience in the T. S. included cases like the B. T. S. I have found the course I advise to be the best and only one.

You cannot master opposition — *in the T. S.* — by opposition, but only by calm, quiet and persistent attention to your (the B. T. S.'s) attention to its *own field* and duty.

I am fully acquainted with all the facts about the B. T. S., and with many more in D. C. of which you have not heard and my advice is based on both knowledge and experience. I have had the same thing with my own Branch (Aryan T. S.) and the course I took is what I now advise and it succeeded and we are now some 70 strong — and active.

All assistance and encouragement that I can give will be given to B. T. S., and I will say confidentially as a supposititious case that if another Branch asked me to go to D. C. to help publicly I would only consent when the B. T. S. had joined in the invitation.

With all good wishes
I am fraternally
WILLIAM Q JUDGE

P. S. Further. In fact the more cordially the B. T. S. assists any other Branch then the better for B. T. S. and all others.

Office of General Sec. Amer. Sec. T S

Col H S Olcott,   Mar 14, 1890.

My dear Olcott:

In this I beg to hand you another small contribution of five dollars in sterling. It is from W. C. Temple, a member of the Aryan, and is to be applied by you to general theosophical purposes, and is not intended for the permanent fund. For my part I think if that fund was not donated to it would be better for all — it is better to spend money in advancing the cause than to hoard it up. What is your opinion?

I hope you are well and that you got to India all right, and that you have begun to straighten things out there. They sadly needed something. As a prophecy I will tell you this out of my own head — the headquarters are going to be in better shape soon and the whole affair very encouraging to you and all concerned.

What am I to believe about this charge that there has been stealing at Adyar? I have noticed that some of the sums I have sent over there have never been reported as far as I could see.

Sincerely as ever,

WILLIAM Q JUDGE

Mar 14, 1890

My dear H. P. B.:

It is with great pleasure that I hand you in this another small contribution for yourself from a friend who does not care to be known except as your friend. It is the sum of two pounds more or less. It is quite likely that he will send you a similar sum each month. Accept it and ask no questions.

The E. S. is now in such a state that it seems to me to be absolutely necessary for you to take the next step, and to declare, *or make,* the inner section of it and thus to have those on whom you can rely do the work for the others and at the same time protect the Section from the lot of fools who are now in it. I find that many of them came in just for curiosity and do not care much about the pledge; it is not sacred for them. Some of the copies of No 3 have been lost in the mail because of the failure to tell me of change of address and they will not even answer when I ask about it.

You ought to have *an inner section,* the existence of which is to be known only to those in it, and they should

177

be selected with great care — I can give the names of the sure and careful ones in this country. They will keep all secrets and at the same time should be the only channel for the others — that is to say, the Instructions for the others should come in a mild form from this inner section, for I assure you that the majority of those now in are unfit to have your papers by reason of lack of intelligence and education. Will you not do this? Is it not a new and good method for tightening the grip you have already on the movement and for guiding the people in the right way in theosophy?

I wait to hear.

As ever yours,

WILLIAM Q JUDGE

You to give the real Instructions to the Inner Section only, and that Section to be entered only on your conferring the right and never upon application.

Dear Countess   Ap. 22 1890

Your letter at hand with such sad news of H P B's health. Like you I feel that she will live. The body is really worn out and only kept alive by extraordinary means. The *real one* is now — or was — paralyzing it so that at this crisis the head should not do such work as to cause untimely death. I *know* that if that *one* should be away a moment you would see the body collapse before you. It is sad. But we must hope.

Now as to the money. The $1000 being all in hand I turned over that sum to him and he obtained a London cheque for it from Neresheimer and it has been sent you. It is only a moments work for H. P. B. to sign it and then you can deposit at once.

I only thought to save time by asking for the contract. There is no question of honesty or good faith; it is all pure business and no more.

If, when you get the cheque, H P B should die before it is signed by her, then of course you will send it back at once to Mr. Fullerton as it is personal and not meant for her heirs.

I am awfully rushed as I go to Chicago Convention tomorrow. It is too bad H P B is sick for all sakes as well as her own.

My Love to all.
Sincerely,
WILLIAM Q JUDGE.

———

J. Alban Kite, M.D.   May 2, 1890
    Nantucket, Mass.
My dear Sir:
I have yours of the 25th just received upon my return from the T. S. Convention in Chicago. Your question gives "sin" as the opposite of "truth," but the opposite of "truth" is not "sin" but "untruth," and your question whether sin is recognized as existing *per se* would have to be answered

in the negative, because if it exist *per se* it would never cease to exist; it is a state of relation and not an essentially existing thing, for sin is the lack of conformity to some regulation, hence, when the regulation is conformed to, sin ceases to exist, and as it is only a relative condition it can have no real existence. I must ask you to excuse this short letter, as I am so busy that I really don't know what to do.

Very truly yours,
WILLIAM Q JUDGE
General Secretary

———

Mrs. Mary H. Bowman,   May 13, 1890
  Santa Cruz, Calif.
My dear Mrs. Bowman:
  . . . . If I had any right to dictate in regard to the conduct of Branches, I would say that they should be open and that discussion should be free, and that as little as possible parliamentary law indulged in, as the latter retards freedom and can only be necessary on certain occasions when people need repressing. In the May Path you will find an excellent article by a friend of mine upon the subject of Branch Work. I am,

Very sincerely and fraternally yours,
WILLIAM Q JUDGE
General Secretary

Mrs. L. W. Smith,   May 19, 1890
  Nordhoff, Ventura Co., Calif.
My dear Madame:

I have your long letter and it seems to me that you misunderstand the position of Theosophists in regard to Christianity. Mme. Blavatsky and other Theosophists are not opposed, as you infer, to the teachings of Jesus, quite the contrary, they always insist that his teachings are the same as have been in all ages taught by true teachers. The question whether he ever existed is one which each person decides for himself; personally I do not think any such person ever lived, but that does not prevent me from admiring what he is alleged to have said. But Mme. Blavatsky and every other Theosophist is opposed to the dogmatic teachings of the Churches, and that is what is called by the name of Christianity; and as the Churches have that name, those persons, including yourself, who believe in the teachings of Jesus are not Christians and their beliefs are not attacked in any way by any of us. Furthermore, the Theosophical Society opposes no person's religion and no one is bound by the statements of any individual member on that subject. It seems to me that the grief which you express at the things you dislike in Theosophical writings is due to your own misunderstanding of the true position of the Society and of its leading members. I have been acquainted with Mme. Blavatsky for over 15 years, and although you quote from her writings, yet I know that you misunderstand her position. She has so frequently referred to Christian Bibles and writings because it is necessary to do so when speaking to minds like your own, for instance, who have been educated under the Christian system, for those minds have been by that education set into the Christian groove. The fact that the teachings of Jesus are old and well-known before his time proves nothing in regard to him except that he taught them, but goes to show conclusively that no religious sect can claim exclusiveness or divinity for their particular ideas.

As to "Mind Cure" and "Divine Healing" I would prefer to say nothing, for the reason that I have some convictions of my own on those subjects which seem to me to be based upon scientific law and reasons which are far more far-reaching than those advanced by the votaries of either school. You will excuse a longer letter as I am excessively busy. The price of the Report of the last Convention when it shall be ready will be 25 cents. I am,

Sincerely yours,
WILLIAM Q JUDGE

H. D. Rogers Esq   May 23, 1890
Dear Sir

I have yours of 18th in which you refer to having spoken to me in Chicago "about initiation." Pardon me for forgetting, but I met so many I cannot remember it.

Entering the T. S. is not such a very serious "initiation" and by that word you may mean what I do not. One can belong to the T. S. and yet at the same time to a

Church, and one can always do what is possible to aid others searching for spiritual light.

I do not find your name on our roll. But I do not see why a member of the Church cannot be a good theosophical member. If you wish to join I will give you all needed information and shall be glad to hear from you again.

Very truly

WILLIAM Q JUDGE

Gen Secy

Personal   May 30, 1890

Dear Griffiths:

Your nature like mine is such that with so many elements to meet out your way it is absolutely necessary that you do not permit them to think you are exercising authority and to do that you have to curb yourself as I also. *Verbum sap.*   Sincerely

WILLIAM Q JUDGE

Mrs. A. F. Smith restored

Mr. William Throckmorton,   June 11, 1890

St. Louis, Mo.

Dear Brother Throckmorton:

I have yours of June 9th. The first question which you raise in regard to saloon-keepers being admitted to the Society, it seems to me can be easily solved. The Society has not declared against saloon-keepers, and my opinion is that any person who is not a convict or of known immoral character should be admitted. Neither do I see that we can distinguish against policemen. Nor do I see why it is necessary for any of us to approach any class of men about whom we intend to raise any question. It does not seem to me that the claims made by *some* as to the moral character of these men is of the slightest consequence, unless they prove immorality. As Mr. Fullerton just says, if these people want to come into our Society it must be from a good motive, because it is not a movement which attracts people through any other than a good motive, which is to improve or to improve others. As to going amongst the poor and uneducated, every man must follow his own conscience. Yet, I do not think that we will be able, nor is it necessary, to make converts amongst the classes to which you refer, and of course I agree with your opinion that "The whole of mankind is eligible to attempt at least or to help build the institution on earth, and they should be given a chance"; but you seem to have failed to observe that the chance is given, in the very fact that our Society exists and offers itself to man. There is another thing that we should remember, and that is that our doctrines as yet are very difficult, for the reason that the majority of people have never had any education of that sort.

I do not know anything about the cutting which you enclose and which I return, except that Dr. Schwartz is a member-at-large of the T. S.; about his towering intellect I know nothing.   Sincerely yours,

WILLIAM Q JUDGE

Mrs. Elizabeth A. Kingsbury, Pres^t.   July 3, 1890
  Los Angeles, Calif.
My dear Madame:
  I very deeply regret to hear, from recent communication from Los Angeles, that there exist some complications between the Los Angeles Branch and the other two Branches in your city concerning the establishment of a Headquarters for work. In any city where several Branches exist, it seems most desirable that, while the Branches retain their separate existence and organization, there should nevertheless be some arrangement for united work, whereby loss of time and labor is saved, and also that some Headquarters should be established as a common ground for Theosophic effort. I have been especially desirous to see this effectuated in Los Angeles because of the great success attending a like effort in San Francisco. Such union for common work is wholly within the province of the Branches concerned, and needs no permission from the General Secretary or the Executive Committee, nor has any such been either solicited from or given by this office, much as the project for a Headquarters meets with my own approval.
  It seems to me that the principles bearing upon such a matter are entirely clear. In the presence of a great opportunity for Theosophical work, all past dissensions, all present grievances, if any, and all personal and Branch jealousies should wholly disappear. The firm will to exclude such is one of those opportunities and tests of true Theosophic spirit which encounter the Theosophist as he goes along the Path. His success in subordinating all personal

185

feeling to a sense of duty and a spirit for labor measures the degree in which he has truly progressed as a Theosophist. This is equally true of the Branches. A Branch which hesitates to co-operate with another, or which sets up a Headquarters from which other Branches are excluded, thereby violates the spirit of Theosophy and contradicts the very idea expressed in the name "Headquarters." Anything like two rival Headquarters would be much worse than an absurdity; it would justify outside criticism as well as immediately hinder the work. Indeed, such action would be ground for complaint to the Executive Committee and even to the Convention, unless the action was based upon the refusal of excluded Branches to bear their share of expenses. It is not necessary that Branches should lose their separate existence, but only that they should lose any spirit of isolation, of jealousy, or of hostility. It is with them as with individuals: each person can preserve his own convictions and his own methods of thought, while cooperating with other individuals in common work, and while giving up everything that savors of mere selfish assertion.

It seems to me that the present occasion is one peculiarly appropriate for the permanent burial of all past dissensions or discord, and for the cordial and harmonious union of all Los Angeles Theosophists in the establishment of a strong and active Headquarters. Each participant may very possibly have something to concede in the way of personal feeling. Very well: let him then make that concession as one of the most important gifts he can contribute to Theosophy, and as being the immediate personal duty which Theosophy lays upon him at the moment. If that duty takes the shape of forbearance, patience, conciliation, still very well. The fruits of such are always abundant. It would be a mistake in any one to refuse so to act because another acted differently, inasmuch as there is no reason why one person should fail alike in duty and in reward because another has so failed. But I do not see any reason why any one in Los Angeles should fail. There is only required a firm disposition towards a straightforward and manly course, and then the way opens of itself.

I think, therefore, that each Branch should proffer to the others its cordial cooperation in the establishment of a Headquarters for united work. If any Branch is rejected by others, it at least has done its duty, and may patiently abide the time when the mistake will be seen by the others and spontaneously rectified. Meantime it would not be wise to establish a rival Headquarters or to do anything that would give the appearance of resentment or antagonism. It would be better, I should say, simply to continue the existence and work of the Branch, avoiding all occasions or expressions of irritation, and letting time and patience do their perfect work. This policy is in accordance with human nature and with the known operations of higher law.

If, in the pursuance of the policy of duty, any one finds discouragement or pain, this is not to be wondered at, for such experiences we encounter in many relations in life. But it would be a great mistake to allow such discouragement to drive one from the field of immediate duty, or to operate in any other way than to fortify the resolution to

187

continue faithful to the end. This very endurance may be one of the sacrifices which are to be offered by the personality towards the Cause of Theosophy.

I shall be very glad if you will express these views to other members of the T. S. in Los Angeles, and, if you approve, read this letter to your Branch. You must understand that I speak with no tone of authority, and with absolutely no wish to constrain any fellow member, but as an old Theosophist who has seen much of the workings of human nature in the Society, and who has had ample proof that every sincere effort is helped by Higher Powers, so that I may without impropriety give my brethren the advantage of what I have learned in these years of experience. I think you will all see the justice of these suggestions as you patiently consider them. With kind salutations to all F. T. S. in your city, and with the most cordial wish that all past troubles may abate and that every one may unreservedly unite in the great opportunity now opened for concerted work, I am,

Always faithfully and fraternally yours,
WILLIAM Q. JUDGE

I have mailed to Miss Off the June Lucifer.

Mordecai D. Evans, Esq.   July 3, 1890
    Cape House, Cape May
Dear Bro. Evans:
    I have no doubt you are right in surmising that Coues
is, as you say, meditating an attack on H. P. B., for it is
only by attacking the great that the little are ever heard
of. But as for myself I learned 4 years ago from H. P. B.
to take no steps and no precautions about Mr. Coues. He
is very thoroughly watched by those who know more and
see farther than he or I; and I never trouble about him
except to feel sorry that a bright intellect like his should
be surrounded by such ominous clouds as are about him;
and for him I am sorry when he shall take his short-
sighted steps. I thank you all the same. This letter is not
confidential.
                                 Sincerely
                            WILLIAM Q JUDGE

———————

Harry S. Budd, Esq.   July 7, 1890
    El Paso, Tex.
My dear Budd:
    I have your extraordinary letter, in which you inno-
cently ask me to define the undefinable; i.e. the relations
of parentless, non-dimensional space to SAT. It cannot be
done, to my knowledge, by any mortal this side of Nirvana. But is it not clear enough to you, from the state-

ment in the "*Secret Doctrine*," that space must, in itself be SAT? You cannot do away with the idea of space. If you imagine all the atoms, however compounded, as being condensed into one mass existing in space, and then with your mind's hand, sweep them all away, what will be left? — *Space*. Now as SAT is the word whereby we express the idea of Be-ness, and as Space still is, no matter what we do, then it seems to be the case that SAT is the metaphysical expression of Space. These distinctions arise from the necessities imposed upon us by our finite consciousness. Is this clear to you? If not, you will kindly write me what is the doubt.

Yʳˢ fratʸ

WILLIAM Q. JUDGE

Dear Bro Stiles   New York, July 8 1890

I have your answers and therewith enclosed the $2.00 donation to E. S. for which thanks. It seems that the whole concern is poor; it was always thus, and so we must be former good men working out bad karma.

Sincerely

WILLIAM Q JUDGE

190

New York, July 12 1890

The pronunciation of the word is a good thing in groups or individuals *provided* ALL are in harmony and not full of evil or of angry thoughts. *Therefore* as it is difficult to know the condition to be existing it is better not for the present to use it in groups; let the individuals use it themselves, following at the same time the caution uttered by H. P. B. in the Instructions.

In groups it is very likely to be used too cursorily; caution and time to see whether groups are harmonious in reality should be used.

WILLIAM Q JUDGE
Sec to H P B

Bro Griffiths will read this and then hand it to Dr J A Anderson.

W. Q. JUDGE

———

N. Y. July 14 1890.

My dear Mrs Gahan:

I have your letter which perfectly agrees with Mr. Proper's received the other day. I would if I could remove all bad impressions from your mind but you can easily see that I alone am not able and it is always a very bad thing for strangers to meddle in family affairs.

But, as I have known Mme. Blavatsky intimately many years and know all about her work and being myself engaged in it also, I think that you ought at least to give my statements more force than the wild ideas about her that have come up in your mind. You are doing the same about her as many others do without the shadow of cause. You might as well say that Jesus Christ and all the churches are responsible for all the lunatics who have gone mad on religion. Yet neither he nor the churches have anything to do with it.

In the first place I know personally that Mme Blavatsky never wrote a line to Dr Gahan first because I asked her and second because I asked him. If Mrs. Sherburne, a hysterical woman, and an indiscreet young man, dealing nonsensically in mysterious words choose to write to Dr Gahan and to say they do it by order of H. P. B. you must not blame her, but them for improperly using her name. They might just as well have used my name or yours. And you must not say that Mme Blavatsky has a scheme for breaking up families, first because it is untrue and second because it is a legal libel.

There is no one in the U. S. so interested and actively working for her as I am and she has not broken up my family. She has constantly said in public and private that no man should desert his duties in life or fail to carry them out; and as against your charge on her I can point you to 50 families where the husband and wife study theosophy together. And theosophy is pure christianity when rightly understood. Perhaps if you had taken trouble to seriously find out what Dr Gahan was finding in theosophy and helped him in it you might have aided him much, aided yourself much and prevented annoyance. I do not give advice but only suggestion, and speak from experience. It is natural when a wife sees only wrong (without any examination) in what her husband believes that their relations should become strained. I do not know that this kind of language will suit you but it is sincere and founded on some twenty years of observation of such facts and circumstances.

As for Mr Keightley, he is a very earnest and self-sacrificing young man. He has as much money as anyone could wish and the right to move in what the world calls in England good society, yet he is devoting himself to work in an organization where he gets more trouble than pleasure I assure you. Hence your first suspicion of him that he was on a begging tour was groundless. I think he was foolish to have anything to do with Mrs Sherburne's letter to Dr Gahan but that is a mistake anyone would make and has nought to do with your troubles.

If you continue to harbor the thought about Mme Blavatsky which is expressed in your letter thus: "I have always thought she would do some harm to us," why always you will twist every little circumstance so as to work against her.

Now I believe I can say no more except to solemnly repeat that Mme Blavatsky has had no more to do with your troubles and with that letter than the babe unborn; and that I think the fluid you speak of was simply water and nothing else.

Perhaps if you tell Dr. Gahan to go somewhere else for a year — say to N Y and open practice — so that his mind shall ease off since the cause of his jealousy seems to him to be in Nebraska, it would do good. It certainly will be better than keeping him there and fighting him.

Sincerely

WILLIAM Q JUDGE

Dear Bro Fulkenstein   July 30, 1890

Your letter remains confidential. Your case is not a rare one. All students who are sincere pass through hard trials; else how could they grow strong? You have fallen into the sphere of doubt. This is doubt of yourself and therefore dark and appalling. If you fight it with determination it will pass away. It is in your case one of the effects of the pledge fever, and therefore, as it is an inner defect coming to the surface you ought to accept the chance to root it out, for if it had remained within you would never know it was there and hence never attack it.

It is not necessary for you to blindly accept the teachings; but on the other hand it is wholly unnecessary and injurious to *reject* it merely because your mind is in its present state. There is a great distinction here. You should therefore suspend conclusions upon points you do not grasp.

But more important than all else is it that your life should coincide as far as it can with your own beliefs. This anyone can cause to come about. We are all weak and often fall and our duty is to rise from each failure, no matter how many, and try again. Is not this easy. Is it not easy to be a small star if we cannot be a great planet? and after a time you will see more clearly what to do.

Now my advice is that if you continue as at present you had better go out of the group for a while. If you so wish I will transfer you and place the matter for you before the others in its right light.

Let me hear from you again.

Sincerely,
WILLIAM Q JUDGE

194

Dear Bro Rumford: New York, Aug 6 1890

. . . . I notice this in your letter: "and growing through study of and conflict with Elementaries." If your [words] express the same ideas for you as they do for me then you are playing with a dangerous thing. The study of Elementaries is in reality the study of devils; they were always called devils in the old days. I should drop it if I were you and wait.   Sincerely

WILLIAM Q JUDGE
Sec to H. P. B.

————

Box 2659
Dear Bro Rumford   N Y Aug 8 1890

I have your letter. I must talk seriously and beg you to take what I say in good part. Your reply that you have signed the pledge and *keep it* is astonishing in the face of the printed plain directions that you are to write it out sign the written one and send it to me, keeping the card yourself for reference. But if you have written it out and sent to London that is equally against the directions you received. This signing of the pledge is the first step and the manner in which it is taken is an index for you and for me as to you. This Section is accurate and scientific, and while many inaccurate and unscientific persons are in it still they only progress in reality by accident as it were, for inattention and inaccuracy preclude progress in the higher paths just as much as they do in this world. In this

195

school nothing is by accident nor by favor and if we are attempting to know this highest knowledge we must have all the habits demanded in science. It is only the sincere, devoted, attentive and accurate ones who get ahead. Now in your case you have apparently paid no attention to the directions. Will it be the same further on? That is for yourself to answer to yourself. I require no answer as I am not the judge —

As to the other matter. You will not cure the boy by taking on his symptom. If you wish to cure him you must try and in addition get him to take hold himself you meanwhile helping him by strong will and magnetism. If this vicarious method of yours were the one then the great Adepts could in a day cure humanity by the same process. But you see they do not: humanity has to struggle on as ever in misery until they acquire self mastery and self knowledge. It may be hard but it is the law.

Sincerely yours

WILLIAM Q JUDGE

Geo. H. Stebbins, Esq.   Aug. 11th, 1890
   National City, Cal.
Dear Bro:

I have yours of the 3d, in which you say that you think it would be well to have a school or institution for the teaching of Theosophical knowledge, in California, and asking my opinion. What Mme Blavatsky says, as quoted by you, seems to meet the case for she refers to the establishing of a centre of activity in Theosophical work in California.

The establishment of a college, or of a seat, where teaching in Theosophy should be given is, in my opinion, premature, for the reason that at present we are all learners and not yet real teachers. If a college were established it would not result in entire good, but would probably increase dogmatism of another character. The establishment, however, of a centre of activity (and all the better in a settled place) would be well, because it would form a focus for the spreading of information regarding Theosophy and its literature, and would not be open to the objection to which a school or college would be subject. Such a "Headquarters" exists in London, another in India and a small one here. The more we have of these, the better. I could elaborate these views more fully, but just now am extremely busy as Mr. Fullerton is away.

Yours fraternally
WILLIAM Q JUDGE

Mr. C. L. Robertson,   August 11, 1890
 Duluth, Minn.
Dear Brother Robertson:

I have your letter of the 7th. The absence of Mr. Fullerton on his vacation crowds me with work, so that I cannot reply at the length I would wish. I agree with you that we should battle with our pen for the T. S. Your informant, Mr. Ellerson, is guilty of falsification in what he told you. He has absolutely no knowledge, and his assertion that he was present and knew anything is a lie. The facts are briefly these: — Col. Olcott met Mme. Blavatsky in Vermont in '74. Afterwards in '75 he and she resided, it is true, in the same flat in New York, but their acquaintance was proper and his sister resided there also. I am in business with his brother, know his sister, all his relatives. His character has always been good. He was not induced to leave his family at all. He has two sons, now grown men, and gave them a good education and a start in life. I myself attended to part of this for him long before he met Mme. Blavatsky. It is true he was divorced from his wife, but that was before he ever heard of Mme. Blavatsky, and she married again a man named Cannon. He never had four children. At the time he left New York one son had already been placed by him in business in California, and the other was just leaving college. You can see what lies this man you speak of is guilty of when he accuses Olcott of desertion. These facts which I give you are known to hundreds of persons in this city, friends and acquaintances of the family, and it has always been well-known that he permitted the divorce in order to satisfy Mrs. Olcott who did not care for him and who has always been blamed, even by her own relatives. Since 1875 Olcott's career has been public in India, and can be found all through the "Theosophist," the New York "Sun," and other publications. This is about all I can say at present.

Fraternally yours,

WILLIAM Q JUDGE

Wᵐ Throckmorton, Esq   Aug. 12ᵗʰ 1890.
Dear Sir and Brother:

Your letter to hand and I am glad to see how much work you have done in sowing the seed. Owing to the absence of Mr Fullerton, I am pressed for time and must be brief. It is well to say to those who ask what benefit they can derive from joining T. S. that (a) they are thereby enabled to work in and through an organization established for the ethical aid of others and (b) through this Society they can better obtain aid from the inner planes of being, such real aid not being drawn from books. The real Founders of the T. S. help those in it who help others, such help being the main purpose of its establishment.

I have sued the Sun, but am at present letting Coues alone. Have also entered suit for Madame Blavatsky. Very little, if any harm has been done so far as we now see.

Hastily but fraternally yours,

WILLIAM Q JUDGE

———

Mr. R. M. McKee   Aug 12ᵗʰ, 1890.
Greenville, Tenn.
Dear Sir:

Your favor of the 8ᵗʰ inst is received and the book asked for has been sent you, viz: Occult World Phenomena. Your views in regard to methods of instruction are clearly put and accord with my own in the main, but the book reviewed has little real information in it and is not of value to the earnest student, in my opinion.

199

Dhyan Chohans are progressed beings who have passed through human and all the other stages of life. Upon reaching perfection as Men and Adepts, they have then gone on to still higher conditions which we can hardly conceive. They are above Nirvana, in the sense that they have long ago earned the right to it, but have chosen to remain where they can still assist Humanity. In the next pralaya they will go into Nirvana and, when that period is over, they will emerge, passing on to higher spheres and conditions of which we have now no idea. The evolutionary ladder is endless. Note also that a man may be in devachan or in Nirvana while still in the body, if he has purified his soul, for these are states and not places. The questions raised by you indicate the necessity for a closer study of Isis, the Secret Doctrine and kindred.

Very truly yours,
WILLIAM Q JUDGE

————

Col. H. S. Olcott,   Aug 13, 1890
    Adyar, Madras, India
My dear Olcott:

By this mail I send you in a separate box the pin of the Theosophical Society according to the design which we agreed upon in 1875. One of our recently acquired members in New York is a jeweler, and having heard about the pin he made several for us of different sizes, and this one I procured as a present to yourself. I think you will like it and I hope you will wear it. If you find any members in India wishing to have some, we are taking steps to have them made, enameled on silver instead of on gold, so that they will cost only about $1.25. The present one which I send you is more costly and could not be sold to any advantage in India.

I heard from London yesterday about Mr. Fawcett's defection. I may say that I expected it from my perusal of his writings, because there were certain evidences in his works which led me to suppose that he was more intellectual than otherwise and that he could not stand the concentration of forces which one is sure to meet and that in loneliness at Adyar. It has been my opinion for a long time that in all cases where new people offer themselves, it is much wiser to let them do what they can and not persuade them to any great extent until we are sure that they will stick. I am sorry that I made such a parade of Mr. Fawcett's lectures in the Path, although, to tell the truth, my feelings were against it and I was rather carried away by Fullerton's persuasions.

Hoping you are well and that you will be satisfied with the new help which is going out to you, I beg to remain,

Sincerely as ever,
WILLIAM Q JUDGE
Gen Sec

Col. Henry S. Olcott,   August 18, 1890
My dear Olcott:

I have just had your letter and am glad that the money I sent came in at the right time. Now I want to say, and hope you will agree with me, that the policy of keeping up a permanent fund does not seem to me to be a good one. It is rather in the nature of disbelief in fate and the future. I am satisfied that the future will be all right, and think that keeping a lot of money like that unused when we need money so much is bad policy, and that if we used it for the purpose of doing more work and broadening the lines of influence of the T. S. it would be a better investment for the future than keeping it at interest. It may be very nice to leave money to your successors, but I question whether they will be able to use it to the same advantage of the Society as you could in your lifetime. I hope that you will take some steps to release the fund.

Now there is another sort of permanent fund in which I have a great interest, and that is a fund of activities begun, energies brought out, and influence extended, which will redound one-hundred fold in the future and which ought to be centered in Adyar. You will allow me to say from an intimate knowledge of the facts that up to the year '86 when I began here again, very little, if anything, had been done by the Indian centre for American T. S. interests, and I can tell you as a fact that up to that time and up to very recently many persons here when asked to aid India replied "What has India done for us, anyhow!" Basing this remark upon the fact that the office

202

in India, whatever the reason, had made themselves very little known to Americans. If the contrary had been the fact and if little activities of various sorts had been started at the Headquarters, designed especially for America (and which has been my effort here), I think you would have found a more constant and sincere support from Americans than you have had. That which you have begun to have is directly due to our efforts here on that line. But I do not think it is too late to commence, and I shall be willing to aid you in it, because, notwithstanding what Mr. Harte or other persons may have said, my attitude internally and aim has been to make India the real centre of this movement, as it ought to be. This idea does not clash at all with the present scheme of administration, which can be kept up. India is somewhat of a mystery to the majority of people here and could be made a great factor in their lives and thoughts. At present the great centre of thought for them in America is this office, which really, as you know, has nothing in it but devotion. I wish you would think this over as I shall be doing for the next month, and any suggestions you may have, send me at once, as I shall also send to you, and perhaps we can arrive at some plan. But I must impress upon you my desire that you should not talk this over with other persons, and especially not with those who have been in India and made trouble there. But in Bert Keightley you will find one who agrees with me. I shall do my best of course, always to get you what help I can, and I may say that just as soon as I was able I sent you assistance and would have been able to send it before, had it not been for the indifference and cantankerousness of certain persons not in this country, and also in some degree because of your own leaving America to itself when you had a big opportunity with men and traditions behind you to use.

Aff^y and Fraternally yours,

WILLIAM Q JUDGE

Mr. Peter Long   August 21, 1890
    St. Paul, Minn.

As to Mr. Keightley he made explanation which showed him in a favorable light. We cannot go on forever refuting vile slanders. As to H. P. B. there have been said against her for fifteen years many things worse than that by Dr. Coues and if her work and her works are not her recommendation and justification then any other than her suit upon the Wittgenstein story cannot be attempted. There are enough stories (lies) told of her and Col. Olcott to damn them twice over. Personally I care nothing about them believing them untrue and have too short a time to live with too much to do in that space to darken my work at the bidding of loafers and liars like this slandrous El Coues.

WILLIAM Q. JUDGE

[The above paragraph was appended by Mr. Judge to a letter addressed to Mr. Peter Long by Alexander Fullerton, August 21, 1890]

Mr. Harrie S. Budd,   August 24, 1890
   El Paso, Texas
Dear Sir:

I have yours of the 8th in which you proceed with your questions. I did not stumble on the word "relative." Relativity is something which we all have to study, since by it alone are we able to know anything with certainty. The fact of the matter is that there is no relation between "space" and "sat" whatever, consequently there is no necessity in inquiring what the relation may be. I think it would be impossible to answer the question: — "What is the relation between N- or infinitely dimensional space and absolute space," because they must be the same thing; hence there can be no relation. The word *parent-space* in the "Secret Doctrine" is probably only a mere term in order to get the mind to fix itself upon space as the universal parent, so to speak. Indeed, it is unwise to speculate upon the relation of the absolute to anything, and it will be found to be a source of danger to the mind. It is true that 1, 2, 3, etc. are born from that which is *not*, because we are incapable of comprehending *it;* hence we have to be satisfied with beginning with 1. I think it is an error to say that "the evolution of space progresses," for no dimension whatever is added to it, but our perception of certain relations obtaining in space are added to our consciousness or to our possessions. Therefore, at all times, space is either dimensional or undimensional, just as you please. You have hit upon a very high metaphysical question and the sooner you satisfy yourself upon the subject on the lines indicated by me, the better it will be. It follows, therefore, that space does not come back to the condition of non-dimension, but that as our consciousness is increased or enlarged we perceive that space ever *is,* and that dimensions arise solely from difference in location, so to speak, of the consciousness. In the "Bhagavad Gita" you will find that Krishna says "Try to understand this my supreme mystery. I am in all these things and I am not; I am connected and I am not connected." Now I may ask you in your own words "Does this make it clearer?" I have not taken your words literally, and must ask you not to take mine so.

Sincerely

WILLIAM Q JUDGE

Dr. Franz Hartmann,   September 2, 1890
 Vienna, Austria
Dear Doctor:

I have received yours of August 21st just upon my return from the country. I shall print your letter next month under Correspondence, but as it is rather long shall take a little out, but not much. As far as concerns your letter I think you are quite right in the main that very few people understand the meaning of the term "self-knowledge." At the same time I think you are carried away by the desire to make those who cannot understand this term possessors of that wisdom. They have to be brought up gradually to that point, and I think such is the work of the T. S. Those who, like yourself, have arrived at an understanding of the term "self-knowledge" and of what practical Occultism consists, can be very well left alone by the T. S. because they do not need its assistance, having probably gone beyond it. I would like to write you a longer letter, but am simply overcrowded with a mass of correspondence which accumulated in my absence.

Sincerely yours,

WILLIAM Q JUDGE

———

Mr. I. B. Rumford,　　　　　　　　　September 3, 1890
　　Camden, N. J.
Dear Brother Rumford:

I have your long letter of the 22nd about my suit against "The Sun," enclosing the Golden Gate Resolutions which I return to you. It is not possible for me to give you my views at length, because I am so very busy. But to speak briefly, I may say that your view amounts to pushing the doctrine of Universal Brotherhood altogether too far. We cannot hope to form a Universal Brotherhood: our object stated is that our desire is to form the *nucleus* of one. All life is a compromise and a violation of Universal Brotherhoods. It is one of the paradoxes of nature. I occupy a position in business where I am making money; necessarily by holding that position I prevent some other equally worthy person from making that money; when I breathe and eat I cause the death of myriads of

207

beings — yet were I to push Universal Brotherhood to its extreme limit, then I should have to die at once. This question really is one relating to a person's inner attitude. If I should fight unnecessarily, it is wrong. If even when fighting necessarily for the protection of the Society and its members against attacks now and in the future I should still have personal feelings, to that extent I would then be wrong too. But I have no such personal feelings. I feel just as much pity for "The Sun" and for Coues as you do, but my duty says that inasmuch as vile attacks have been made upon the Society, using me as the prominent person, I have to repel those attacks in the only way provided by our civilization, that is in the Courts. Were we to allow these people to escape on the ground that Universal Brotherhood demands it, then we are using the doctrine to injure the hundreds who have been damaged by the libel, merely that we may protect the vile creature such as Coues, and an equally vile newspaper. Such a course would be unjust, and we must not let ourselves forget our duty to all, which might happen when we consider our relations to one or two individuals. This is all I have to say at present.

Fraternally yours,
WILLIAM Q JUDGE

Mr. William L. Ducey,   September 5, 1890
    Muskegon, Mich.
Dear Brother Ducey:
    I have yours of the third. I think it is not well for you
to adopt the method of statement which you ask my advice
about. It is very true that when persons say "I" and "my,"
they are impelled to do so by the lower personal element
which is what we know as the false "I," in other words the
present personality. But when they say "Is my soul im-
mortal?" or "Will it be saved?", they are referring to the
individuality, because they are not able yet to distinguish
between the perishable and the imperishable soul. Hence
I disagree with you when you say as follows: "It is my
belief that the ordinary man or woman means this personality, this self, when they speak of their soul." Therefore,
when they ask you if their soul will survive the death of
the body, you should say Yes, waiting until such time as
they have the larger knowledge and are able to see that
the soul may be destroyed, and, as you know that even this
destructible soul persists for immense periods of time before it can be destroyed. You should also revise the statement expressed as follows in your letter: "I think it a rare
event for a soul to be saved" and alter it that "You think
it a rare event for any particular soul to reach perfect
liberation in any particular life," because when a soul steps
upon the Path toward liberation definitely, it consumes
many subsequent incarnations before it reaches liberation.
    If I have not fully answered your queries, please ad-
vise me.   Sincerely yours,
                        WILLIAM Q JUDGE

Dr. J. S. Cook,   September 9, 1890
    Sacramento, Calif.
Dear Brother Cook:
    I have yours in which you speak of a desire to study
the third object of the Theosophical Society. You ask me
for my sincere advice, and although I am in years a
younger man I will give it, as it is based upon a very wide
experience in the matters to which you refer. You having
seen many days are able to receive the truth frankly, and
the very first thing to state is this, which has been not
only asserted by learned sages but also proved in my experience, that, after a man passes forty, it is not only difficult but dangerous to study in the line of psychic effort.
This line is surrounded with deception and danger. The
deception is within and therefore extremely difficult to
understand. Besides that it is an absolute law and absolute fact that psychic attainments disappear when the body
dies, and for that reason even a lifetime spent in that pursuit is to some extent wasted. Psychic powers are not and
never were the object of those who may be called Adepts
and who possess such powers, but are mere incidentals
occurring from the exercise of knowledge and the centre
of power. They are just the same as the movements of
the joints, of the muscles, and the nerves when we walk or
otherwise act. Now such movements are not our object,
but our object is the accomplishment of an act, the movements being incidental to that accomplishment. But the
sincere study of the spiritual philosophy (I do not mean
spiritualism) is actual progress, because all that is acquired in that is never lost with death but remains and
210

comes back on rebirth. Furthermore, I scarcely believe that you have an idea of the tremendous difficulty in pursuing psychic studies, per se, of the discrimination, the power, the determination, the bodily force, the energy, the clearness of sight required for such practice. These things called mediumship, clairvoyance, and so on, as commonly exhibited, are only little specks on the whole, mere fleeting illustrations of what the real thing is, and as you know, almost always occurring with untrained persons who do not understand them. My sincere advice therefore is to continue in the path which leads to spiritual knowledge, for as Krishna says in the "Bhagavad Gita," "Spiritual knowledge includes every action without exception."

Fraternally yours,

WILLIAM Q JUDGE

———

Important.

Dear H. P. B.   Sept 12 1890

I want to lay before you again the matter of our having over here some hindu upon whom we can rely to work for the T. S. *with me.*

First. Can such a man be properly selected from among hindu theosophists in London by you and the english F. T. S. without the necessity of my going to London for that purpose?

If it is absolutely necessary I can get away for the purpose for three or four weeks and bring him back with me.

Second. The selection of a man ought to be with the needs of America in view and not from the english standpoint, either as to public speaking or otherwise. In America a man ought to be able to speak in public. It is a common habit and ability here.

Third. The coming over of a good man would do more to offset the recent scandals and take advantage of them than any thing else we could imagine.

Fourth. And it must be a hindu because a "foreign prophet is best." Hence I do not want Mead or AK or anyone english yet for this purpose specially.

Fifth. For qualifications: he must be able to speak publicly, *must be devoted;* must be somewhat acquainted with Sanscrit — the more the better; must understand and believe in theosophy; must work with and under me and stray nowhere.

Sixth. It is necessary that the idea should be put in practise at once; hence my urgency.

I do not care how much glory he may get here — that will be his Karma and temptation — so long as he will carry out our plans and work strictly for the T. S. only.

If he backed away it is to be understood he goes away at once.

Seventh. I guarantee to pay his passage here and back again to London, and to keep him while here. This is all settled and certain, and I can make it good with cash by sending the money from here.

Now two things are important, 1, to do this selecting with care, and 2, *at once.* If there is no hindu in London who can fill this bill of course that settles it.

212

The careful selection is in order not to get a man who merely would like to get to U. S. and then slip off into something else or with somebody else; and also to find one who while knowing Theosophy and Sanscrit is capable of expounding it. I can with such a person push the T. S. and its doctrines and literature all over as we are now in the public eye. Clothing and all necessaries I will provide as reasonably required.

———

On receipt and after you have thought this over telegraph me as to either state of the case.

If no such man can be got you can say "no hindu available."

If one you are sure of on all points is found say:

"Have hindu (giving name)" and we will then forward funds at once it being understood he is ready to start. If you cannot make selection without my presence in London then telegraph

"Judge necessary" and I'll come at once.

———

We have looked all over this matter and consider this step very important in our present situation, and particularly its quick accomplishment.

An extra brilliant man is not necessary we need hardly say from our old experience with Mohini. At the same time we do want common sense and no folly in the man who may come.

As Ever

WILLIAM Q JUDGE

Mrs. A. M. Wyman: Sep 15, 1890

It is not advisable to increase the E. S. too quickly nor to try and get people in. They join too quickly as it is and without having enough acquaintance with exoteric theosophy.

As to a Pres^t the group should do as it likes. It is not an honor but only for convenience and to fix responsibility. One who seeks to have it should not be allowed to have it.

Read this to Group.

                                 Yours
                                 WILLIAM Q JUDGE
                                            Sec

———

                                                    Sep 20, 1890
Dear Bro Rumford:

Some few things you say cause me to agree with you that it will be better for you to *suspend* activities for a while in the E S. You say you had "no idea it was a study and it is hard for you to remember." It is in fact the very hardest study in the world and no man will get on any other way; and also no one can get on if memory is bad. This is true everywhere and more so in spiritual matters than any. But no one can really leave the Section after once entering as you have with your eyes open. You read the rules beforehand and as I supposed with close attention. So my opinion is you had better send me back the papers except rules and pledge; those you should keep by you; and let the matter rest in abeyance until later.

214

You will then remain on the record but I will enter a memo. not to send you papers. This is my sincere judgment. I have long studied these things; I know how hard they are; I know about spiritualism and christianity; and with this knowledge am convinced you are not ripe to go on with studies. But you can still go on in sincerity as an earnest man devoted to the good of humanity to the best of your ability.

Yours
WILLIAM Q JUDGE

I will be away from N Y until next Friday.
The mistakes in the book are due to bad binding.

Dear Bro Hastings   25 Sep 1890

I have yours. I cannot alter the Rules. In the 1st place spirituous liquors are a direct obstacle to any progress in the E S. and hence there are some who must use them who wish to enter the E S but therefore cannot. It would be unwise for you at your age to enter this section for there is no sense in going against nature; you would be undertaking a load which would produce such a reaction on your body that it would succumb altho your inner self would be as ever it was. Secondly we have no desire to interfere between man and wife and I myself think no man should enter the E S. unless his wife does too. It is not merely a new society, but in it great forces are at work that would make the task more difficult than you now imagine. Please send this to W. S. Wing, Omaha Neb who is an E S. officer and correspond with him if you like. Meanwhile you had better return me the papers.

In the exoteric T. S. you can do good and lasting work for the *cause* of humanity for which we should work.

I thank you for photo and shall send on to London.

Sincerely
WILLIAM Q JUDGE

————

New York
Personal   27 Sep 1890
Dear Griffiths

Just read yours about Miss Walsh, the Com^t and Anderson and telegraphed you to wait. It is all right if you do *your* best. Take heart. There is large work to do in E. S. and you can bet you will not be deserted in that without reason — The E S. would take all * man's good work. Just wait and do your best as a mere member. Let the T. S. exoteric try its hand. It was arranged no doubt that Neubauer should make his offer and should have been accepted. With the refusers lies the Karma. Ingratitude is a common human vice but not common to the Masters. Still let Karma work. There is a large lot of spongy brain on the pacific coast. Try to help Walsh so as not to make bad Karma by opposing her, because they selected her by

* indecipherable

216

vote and you must accept that. Keep your present mental attitude.

Perhaps you ought to attend more to business. You are not required to impoverish yourself — Give what time and money you can, but you have an actual duty to your family.

Keep me advised from week to week. Kala, father Time, arranges all these matters.

Sincerely as ever

WILLIAM Q JUDGE

————

Sep. 29 1890

Dear Bro Bowman:

I have yours with $10. enclosed for this Section which I have entered. The statement of a/c was not sent out as a criticism on any one but for information and it showed that the total amount here given was an average of about $2.50 per year.

Regarding the E. S. you are probably right in saying that it is much beyond the most of us who are in it. But such is the material and with that H. P. B. has to work as best she can. As far as selecting goes, it is almost impossible to judge because the occult rule is that all who apply must be given the chance, and on that rule Griffiths has acted. A little more time will show how the matter can be better carried on. It is true many do not grasp the instructions but it is more important they should try to know themselves first of all and that all can try for.

Hence I am obliged to admit those who are not so thoroughly outwardly bad as to be a disgrace.

So much has been said to me about Griffiths I am at sea. He seems to do right as far as I am concerned, and many of those who now criticise him have not been so much in earnest. I do not mean you for your remarks seemed well meant but others about whom I have heard. Still in all of it I have had nothing definite, and I think those who object to him should state *facts* to him, ask him to refer them to me, and then we could have something to go upon. I know how difficult the work is and that the E. S. members as a rule do not give as much attention to simple rules for conduct of business in the E. S. to which they pledged themselves as they would to a business matter involving $10. This is a thing that does not concern intelligence, nor is learning involved in a question of right thought and action as to others. You are the only one who has said anything definite.

Sincerely

WILLIAM Q JUDGE

Sep 29, 1890

Dear Griffiths:

I have your a/c and will enter it. I send you receipt for a/c which you had best show those who paid you.

I read all about it, P. C. Com^t [Pacific Coast Committee] and Miss Walsh. Better accept matters. And also better suggest your view to be that if the P. C. C. intend to ask to be put in the Cons^t it should have no legislative power; but that all Pac. Coast applic. for charters and membership should be ex^d and endorsed by them. Let me know what you discover as to their opinions upon this.

Now for another thing. There seems to be some criticism going on about you and they do not like to complain. Will you tell those whom you know are at it that I have written stating that I know of this and have asked you to ask them to give you a statement of your faults in this matter for you to send to me. I will then have something definite. Just now it makes me tired. Tell me fully yourself your troubles and supposed failings.

Do not worry about Pac. C. Com. Karma will fix it up if you do your duty.

Sincerely
WILLIAM Q JUDGE

Mr. J. J. Fernand,   October 2, 1890
    Los Angeles, Calif.
Dear Brother Fernand:

I have your letter of the 28th of September, detailing some of your work in Los Angeles, and after reading your entire letter, it seems to me that the question at the end, "Was this against union on my part then?" is answered by your letter; and in any case, my dear friend, why is it necessary to ask the question? A true, wise, Theosophist never looks back, but always directly in front. Now, the question is a retrospective one, and according to the rules of Occultism, it is a waste of time, a waste of energy, to either ask the question or answer it. I think you will understand me. There is no past, nor any future; everything is today, in the present, and that which we call the future is really contained in today, and in fact has no real existence; similarly, the past has no existence and is contained, if it be at all, in today. This is no jugglery with words whatever, but is a statement of the absolute and not the apparent fact. So we find in ancient Scripture the caution never to look back, never to be sorry. If we stop to look back, we may find that mistakes of the past assume undue prominence; all we have to be careful about is that every step taken is taken to the best of our ability, with sincerity and purity of motive. The results have nothing to do with us. By pursuing this course we gradually acquire, unconsciously often, the ability to do every thing right, so that the outcome is always greater and greater. This is my answer to your question. If you have had misunderstandings and suffering, I am sorry for it, and I hope you will have no more. All such things as misunderstandings and sufferings are delusions, arising from our own ignorance, and they must occur in one way or another until we leave this world.

It is pleasant news to hear of the possibility of another Branch, but I hope that the new Branch will be a necessity and not a forced growth, because forced growths are always dangerous. Wishing you all success, I remain,

Fraternally yours,

WILLIAM Q JUDGE

Mrs Helen Winsor   Oct 4, 1890
Dear Madam —

I have yours acknowledging receipt of E. S. papers and
note what you say. There is no doubt but that by an
earnest aspiration one arouses all the hidden inner foes,
but then determined effort will destroy them. It is wise
to always remember that "Ishwara" the Spirit that is common to all dwells inside of us and if that be so, our sincere
belief in and reliance upon It will gradually awaken us
to the consciousness that we are that spirit itself and not
the miserable creatures which walk on this earth bearing
our names. Hence I would ever reflect on the spiritual
unity of all beings, continually saying to myself that I am
actually that spirit. Our difficulties are always due to the
personality which is unwilling to give itself up to the great
idea that it has no real existence except in the one Spirit.

Sincerely

WILLIAM Q JUDGE

———

Mr. William R. Savage,   October 7, 1890
    Baltimore, Md.
My dear Savage:

Your fast must now be at an end. I think you have
fasted long enough, don't you?

A fast is a good thing sometimes, but there are times
when it is injurious and may then lay us open to bad results. I think now that you ought to stop fasting as far

as your body is concerned and go to work with a mental fast, meanwhile taking all proper nourishing food which I am sure your mother will procure for you. Now this is my advice to you and I strongly insist that you take it, as I would not like you to get so sick as it seems you will if you continue any longer without good food.

It is one of the great laws of nature that we cannot, while in a mortal body, make any progress if we overtax it. You must remember the old story about the great Buddha who was fasting once very much, when a great Adept came and told him that he was mistaken and must take proper food, because when he was overstraining himself that way the power of his mind and inner self was weakened.

Sincerely yours,
WILLIAM Q JUDGE

Mr. J. J. Fernand,   October 9, 1890.
    Los Angeles, Calif.
Dear Sir and Brother:

I have yours in which you ask me about the matter of a butcher shop next door the Headquarters, and answer it separately as it concerns yourself alone. The other letter will be official in regard to the proposed Branch. I cannot give you any prescription for counteracting the effects to which you refer. If it is a fact that those effects are purely physical, then, no prescription would alter it; but,

222

if, on the other hand, it is purely a mental matter, which I think it is, then a mental prescription will have due effect. One of the main ends in view in Theosophical higher life is that a man should be so strong inwardly that no outward circumstances can have any effect upon his mind or his body. Hence, one ought to take the plain advice given in the "Bhagavad Gita" where Krishna says to Arjuna that he should with equal mind look upon a Brahmin, a cow, an elephant, a piece of wood, a piece of gold, and that he should not be disturbed by any condition whatever which concerns his mortal frame. The reason for this is that our mortal body is simply an illusion, and there is a good deal of fancy by beginners thinking that there are evil effects from the neighborhood of a slaughterhouse. Such evil effects from such a neighborhood are only felt by those who have got, after many years of occult practice, into a certain bodily condition, and then even it is only temporarily. Hence, I should further advise that you should learn inwardly to look at a wholesale butcher shop as one of the ways in which the Supreme Being chooses to manifest himself, and think no more about it. It seems to me that if you do so the blood and flesh will not bother you at all, for you will have arisen above them and they will appear to you as nothing.

In respect to the Path I should be glad to have you take the agency for Southern California, and if you do I will give you the Path for $1.60 per year, that is to say, for subscriptions which you procure and send to me you shall charge $2 per year and send me $1.60. You can begin on this arrangement, and if the results are at all satisfactory, it may be continued. It is understood that this arrangement refers only to such new subscriptions as you send to us.   Fraternally yours,

WILLIAM Q JUDGE

––––––––

Mr. W. D. Hastings,   October 14, 1890
    Kearney, Neb.
Dear Brother Hastings:
    I should be glad to answer your question "What is the cause of asthma" if I really knew. But this is a physical disorder and I am only a lawyer by profession, consequently know nothing about such things. Answering, however, as a Theosophist, I would draw your attention to the fact that the Society is not for the purpose of curing diseases, unless it should happen that people in the course of time, by following its teachings, should become healthy. There is no doubt that all physical derangements arise from inner causes, and I think it is equally true that a sound mind will frequently produce a sound body, though, at the same time, we find unsound bodies holding sound minds. If your asthma is the result of old karmic causes, it is bound to come out; it often comes to men in their later years of life without being constitutional. However, I would follow, if I were you, the prescription you give, which is to allow your spiritual nature to act; still, if I were you, I should not make that the object of my spiritual expansion, because it is in a sense degrading the latter.

Sincerely yours,
224   WILLIAM Q JUDGE

Mr. G. R. S. Mead,   October 23, 1890
   19 Avenue Road, Regent's Park,
     London, N.W., England
Dear Mead:

I have received yours of the 5th which encloses a copy of the Harte interview. Such madness and spite I never saw, and such absurd weakness on the part of Olcott I never expected. One would have supposed that this interview of Harte's would have been replied to by Olcott in such a way as to put him in his right light. I am sorry to say I cannot send a delegate to India nor go there myself, which is what I would like to do.

Sincerely yours,

WILLIAM Q JUDGE

Mr. Richard Harte,   October 23, 1890
   Adyar, Madras, India
Dear Harte:

I have your note enclosed in Col. Olcott's, and by the same mail I have copies of your interviews about Bert in India, and also of your telegrams to him. Inasmuch as these documents are precisely in line with the stuff you have uniformly been sending me for the last year or two, I believe they are authentic. At any rate, if they are not authentic, it remains for you to publicly deny them. You refer to Mme. Blavatsky's occult nose being wrong. I should consider it right, especially in your case, as years ago she told me what harm you would do us and how you would create trouble. Inasmuch as many people think your intentions are good, I am forced to the conclusion that your definition of kindness is spitefulness, and that your power to distinguish right from wrong is absolutely atrophied. In these interviews you have gone to the trouble not only to misrepresent facts but also to make new obstructions and to set in motion false ideas which will have a tendency to involve the Society with the government in India. Col. Olcott's reply to your insane drivel is altogether too mild. He ought to let everybody know that your attack is unworthy of notice, as is that of a man who persistently twists the right into wrong and makes black white. I sincerely trust that you will be deprived of all official position, so that in the future whatever you may choose to say will be devoid of the slightest official sanction. Very truly you are secretary in partibus infidelium. You have hitherto sent me very plain language about myself, and I now give you some about yourself. The best plan for you to pursue is to leave India; leave the Theosophical Society alone. Become a Tipperary Nationalist, anything but to interfere with concerns which you cannot understand. You are a worse enemy to us than Coues is: Coues is no enemy, he is only an outside lunatic who has no power except what we give him, and we give him none; whereas, you have a semblance of authority, remain in the Society, and persist in these outrageous attacks and insinuations, which spring either from lunacy or deliberate malice — you can take your choice. I am writing this way because I know the harm you are doing in India. You can

226

do no harm here, hence, I have no personal concern as to this country in respect to yourself, although you have caused me much annoyance and increased my correspondence by the manner in which you have done some official business with this country. I am,

Sincerely yours,

WILLIAM Q JUDGE

———

Nov 1, 1890

Dear Mrs Wyman

As to colors produced in the way Keightley said and in relation to the Auric Egg, the notice from H P B was distinct that they should be stopped, as the practice at this stage will do harm. You can gain protection by high motive, reliance on the Higher Self and unselfishness in inner attitude. The vision is to be distrusted for those are often produced by the plastic body and also again by black magicians living in the astral light. The safe side is best until you *know*.

As to group. It will be necessary to assign people to the group until it is too large and then another may be made. It *is* pleasant to have a harmonious body but it is our duty to help newcomers to rise to our stage and thus help the whole Section.

Sincerely

WILLIAM Q JUDGE

227

Dear Mrs Hughes: Nov 3, 1890

I have yours enclosing $1 for the E S. I return the letter from Miss Off to you.

All the matters spoken of in yours seem to be old now and perhaps it will be better not to go over them. All I would wish to refer to is the incident given by you of the whole group getting into a very bad state of feeling one to the other and then right in the face of the caution in the Instructions proceeding to pronounce the word. This is just what ought not to have been done then, because then all were out of harmony and the word inevitably laid them open to bad effects. You will remember that H P B has said not to use the word if angry or otherwise with bad feelings.

I sincerely hope that all personal differences have been laid aside and that the group to which you belong is working in harmony. Any group in any place that is out of harmony does some hurt to the whole section. This of course I do not mean in personal sense but only as a reflection upon what is going on from time to time in the whole section. Sincerely yours,

WILLIAM Q JUDGE

———

Dear Bro. Watson: Nov. 5, 1890.

I have yours and am glad to read it. From the very first time I saw your handwriting I knew you were being drawn to Theosophy strongly and expected you would have more trouble than you have had, for the reason that

228

at one time – perhaps not long before you joined the T. S. – you were very much influenced by a stronger mind than yours which caused in you inevitably at a later date, some weakness. It is now your great opportunity to wholly escape from that by taking a firm stand mentally and endeavoring to see the inner meaning of theosophy which is in fact human life.

I congratulate you because introspective experience is the best and strongest.   Sincerely

WILLIAM Q JUDGE

––––––

Nov 5, 1890
My dear Dr Hübbe-Schleiden:

I have yours of 24ᵗʰ Oct. You are at liberty always to translate and reprint anything you wish out of the Path.

The Diary of Chela you speak of is not fiction. I have it. The only thing is that while I called it a diary it was not in that form but more of an autobiographical sketch given me by him with a promise not to show the writing. What is stated, did occur and it is no fiction; and I left out a great [deal] more than I put in. Besides, my dear sir, the term "subjective experience" is misleading. The hearing by the ear of a sound is subjective in essence, as also is the seeing of color. The only objective part of either is the vibration in one case of the auric instrument, and the molecular change in the other of the retina. Do you confuse * or do you allow the word objective to in-

*one line indecipherable

229

clude all of the single phenomena of hearing for instance? Some of the experiences in that diary were of course what is usually called "subjective" in part, but even each one of them had the objective element also for they were translated to the outer consciousness of the person. None of these phenomena could have been seen or reported by the chela unless his objective apparatus had something to do with them.

As to the other part of yours in which you in effect ask me if I can put you in communication with some adept who will and who can help you in the T S movement in Germany, or if I will give you advice what to do in the matter. You do me too much honor in asking me these two things. I am not fit to give advice to you who are more learned and older than I am, for I am now but 39 years old. And hence all I can say will be in the nature of my suggestions made to you solely because you have asked me for them.

The matter has two aspects. One, Are the adepts whom I know of interested in Germany? The other, Has the T S movement yet penetrated to that land? I answer in the affirmative, and yet at the same time I may be in error. But if the philosophy of the occult hierarchies is correct then They must all be interested in each part of the whole family of people on the earth. I have always believed, and on the dictum of H P B, that St Germain was so interested and she intimated to me that he is not dead at all. But on that point I have not much actual knowledge.

The next point is as to the T S. That is a special movement and not the only one with its object for truth is one.

The very adepts who are in it must at the same time have an interest in Germany, but how that is being or is to be exhibited I do not know at all, and it would be presumption in me to surmise. But I do know this, that They always help when any work is being done for the T S in a loyal spirit, and it is here perhaps that one difficulty may be. For if one cannot abide the personality of the woman whom I believe They have chosen for the particular work of the T S, then of course one cannot expect help from Them in Their special attitude of aiders of the T S, however much They may be willing to help a man in other directions. The personality of H P B is and always will be a stumbling block for many persons and if it were not so, and so deliberately, then we would not have a true or even an approach to a true T S, for had she been all that one could wish in the way of loveliness of character then the members would not think for themselves but would bow down and offer to her the worship which it is the object of the T S to root out of the mind of the age. And I have never known the Adepts or Their real agents to make any mistake in the carrying out of their great objects. But They do not refuse to aid a man because he does not agree with Olcott or H P B in method.

Now I believe that any one can come into relations with the occult fraternity but he has to work very hard to do so and must accomplish it by rising to the plane on which they are and not by bringing Them down to his. You know the old proverb or verse that the kingdom of heaven is taken by VIOLENCE. That I believe to be true and the violence has to be of such a nature that it takes the place by storm. There is another word also and that is "try." It also is of great import and has to be pondered on.

All of the foregoing is in the nature of that advice you ask for, and all I can say in conclusion is, that I have sent your request to the only person I can send it to as I have no right and no means of sending messages to the Adepts. If indeed I were given now the boon of asking of Them some thing or other I confess I would not know what to do as I feel that I have not yet used all that has been accorded to me by karma and the lodge.

Hoping that this may be of some service to you, and being willing to do all I can and anything else you may ask which is in my power, I beg to remain

Fraternally yours,

WILLIAM Q JUDGE

Mrs A K Botsford   Nov 11, 1890
Dear Madame

No 3 Aids and Sugs which you lost is out of print and I can only send you the plate.

So many instances have occurred in the E S. of loss of papers by members that I think H. P. B. will be very unlikely to give out any very secret occult matter. In this way the E S. does itself an injury.

Sincerely

WILLIAM Q JUDGE

Mrs. Anna L. Doolittle,   November 14, 1890
    San Diego, Calif.
Dear Madame:

I have read over carefully the article which you sent me by Mr. Merrill and am obliged to return it for the reasons here given, but in the hope that he may later on write something else. There are some fundamental philosophical errors in it to which I beg you will draw his attention.

In the first place it does not seem to me that "Man is the link between spirit and matter." The teachings of all the highest schools of spiritual philosophy are, that man is spirit and not a link between that and something else. Further, it is very plainly held in the "Bhagavad-Gita" and other high authorities that spirit and matter are coexistent, and that the Absolute is neither matter nor spirit, but both together. Now the words for spirit and matter in Sanscrit are Purusha and Prakriti, and it is a noteworthy fact that the name for man in Sanscrit books is also Purusha. Hence, we see that the philosophy classes man by the same name as it does spirit. If we place him and matter together in one class, we then have to say man and matter, thus making a clear distinction between them. It follows then that Man cannot be the link between himself and matter. The link between Man (or spirit) and matter is, if such a thing be possible, the qualities, as they are called in the Hindu books and the Skandas. But there can be no such link in fact, because spirit in its highest acceptance includes all.

The next point is that the paper speaks throughout of

the "perfection and cultivation of the spirit." This is directly contrary to the philosophy, which distinctly holds that spirit cannot be perfected or cultivated, as it is always pure, free, and unconditioned. That which is to be perfected and cultivated is the soul; in other and Theosophical terms, there must be brought about a union between Manas, Buddhi and Atma. It is for these reasons that I do not like to use the paper. It is true that many papers have been used which have not been correct in all respects, but they have always treated upon subjects which were not so fundamental as that of the present paper, which deals with the highest and most vital of Theosophical propositions, from which all the rest flow, and if a wrong basis be laid down, then all that follows will be irretrievably wrong.

Sincerely your friend,

WILLIAM Q JUDGE

Mrs. Zaidee Heath   Nov 17, 1890
    Los Angeles.
Dear Madame:
    I have yours of Nov. 8 in which you refer to this Section, to Mr. Griffiths, to Mr. Keightley and to others in the T. S. in very strong language, without seeming to make the slightest allowance for the failings of human nature common to us all. Upon this however I can pass no criticism but must surely agree with that sentence in your letter which reads: "I was an Occult Student, therefore my

234

Being an E. S. will not affect me much." I have copied it verbatim et literatim. From this of course it must follow that the E. S. is not a body in which you could do good since it is so different from yourself, and especially as those persons against whom you have cause for complaint are members of it. It is desired that it should be as harmonious as possible and that could hardly be when a member is admitted who uses epithets such as "liar and coward" about other members. This certainly is not Theosophy.

The question of age is of no moment to me and I do not care to know how old any one is.

And as to money or prominence, they ought not to have anything to do with admission or rejection of candidates for the E. S.

The whole matter has now grown so old and so surrounded with disputes that I have decided to rule it off the record and anything further that is done will have to be *de novo*.

I have always thought that T. S. members were in too much of a hurry to enter the E. S. which is a much more serious and far reaching step than the most of them believe or know. And if my advice were asked I should say better wait a matter of years than hurry into it.

Fraternally

WILLIAM Q JUDGE

Dear Bro Bowman   Nov 17, 1890

I read yours with pleasure and opened the envelope enclosed with interest and then laughed immoderately. If to forgive is divine then *I* forgive *you* as I hold we are all divine; for the letter sent in the envelope that you return was not strictly E. S. business and need not have on it "private." All of my letters are not private, and I do not think that that letter was on E. S. business. Hence your joke is very good — on you. For I deliberately left off the *private*.

The letter grew out of E S. correspondence but was devoted I think to personal exchanges of personal matters. Am I right or wrong.

I think we thoroughly understand now. I would like to go to Calif and have long been trying to. A pipe in the mouth of Buddha or Jesus would be queer. However neither Fullerton nor I smoke a pipe down here.

Sincerely
WILLIAM Q JUDGE

———

Dear Griffiths   New York, Nov 17 1890

Glad to hear from you and that you take the right view. H P B wrote me one sentence in 1890 and no more private letters "Be more charitable for others than for

236

yourself and more severe on yourself than on others." It is good advice. A strain always weakens the fibres and produces friction.

I hope all misunderstandings will fly away.

As Ever

WILLIAM Q JUDGE

———

Dear Dr Griffiths   New York, Nov 17 1890

I have heard that some Calif members have an idea that the "Word" may be used for material benefit or to bring about material or temporal ends.

Please state to as many as you find this idea in that it is wrong and that such a use of it is Black magic pure and simple and will do them harm. It goes into next Aids E S.

Yours

WILLIAM Q JUDGE

———

Colonel H. S. Olcott,   November 18, 1890
   Adyar, Madras, India
Dear Olcott:

I have been thinking very much over what I have heard from you and others about your proposal regarding a resignation. This rumor as it has reached me is not definite and I do not know that you intend to resign. I want to ask you to throw away my last letter on this subject and substitute this in its place. As I have said previously, there is a strong feeling throughout the U. S. of gratitude to yourself for all your past work, and no one wishes you to resign, but on the contrary, they would all be very much exercised if they had any idea that you intended to do so.

Now, the way I look at it is this, you have been working in India for a good many years very hard in a very bad climate, and this has told upon your nervous system, causing you to show evidences of the wear and tear. The strongest evidence is that you are easily irritated now about matters which in the past never would have irritated you, and in consequence of this you are feeling the effects of various small matters, which make you feel now and then that you had better resign. There is really no cause for a resignation to be found in the general state of affairs, much less so now than there ever was, for things are very much improved and are bound to steadily improve in the future. More especially is this so in the U. S. where I am satisfied there is a great field and which will be bound more and more every year to look at Adyar as its Headquarters, provided of course that centre is conducted so as to arouse their enthusiasm. Now I am satisfied that you are in need of a rest, and furthermore, that it is imperatively necessary that you should take a rest, for a short or a long time — whatever length of time is necessary for recuperation. As it seems to me that some such place as Simla would be a good situation, as I think going to Europe or any other Western centre of activity would increase instead of diminish your present disturbance. You could remain in Simla and now and then if a question

238

arose needing your advice you could give it, meanwhile leaving some other person in charge at the Headquarters, say with the help of an advisory committee and not with the "Board of Control," because the word "control" is very dangerous. This you can state to the Convention, and they will agree with you, and you need not mention the idea of a resignation, but simply say that you are taking a vacation.

The question of money has something to do with this matter, and I am authorized to state as follows, referring you to my previous letter in which I enclosed a draft to cover the expenses of a Hindu who was to come here, and which money I asked you to keep for that purpose even if it took a year to find the man. That sum of money was given to me for the purpose by a friend, and after consulting with him I am authorized to revoke the assignment of the money and to donate it to you personally for the purpose of paying the expense of a vacation, and am authorized also to say that if later on the man about whom I wrote shall turn up we will furnish the money again for that purpose. It is to be understood that the money is given to you for this particular purpose of a vacation, as we think that you need one and that it is quite likely the question of funds has much to do with the matter. The letter in which I remitted you the money was dated September 26th, and I enclosed therein a draft on London for $400. As I sent that to you personally there can be no trouble about your getting it out, since the following are my words on that subject, "I am requested to ask you to place this money on deposit where you can draw it for that purpose when you shall have found a suitable person."

The draft was issued by the Belmonts for 82 pounds, No. 3152, Sept. 26th to your order.

I sincerely hope that you will act on this suggestion, as it will be beneficial to yourself and to all of us, and I shall hope to hear from you very soon about this matter, and also that you shall receive this previous to the meeting of the Convention.

Sincerely yours,
WILLIAM Q JUDGE

———

Dr F B Smith   Nov 26, 1890.
Dear Sir:

You have not carefully read my first reply for if you had followed my advice you would have seen how impossible it is to comply with your request to be initiated as an adept. That is a thing that no man can do for another. And besides you would not have offered me money for it even if it could be done. I must ask you to read the references given in my first letter before we go any further. You cannot get where you may see into the astral light in the way you are seeking for you are seeking on the material plane and this is a matter of the spiritual life. The esoteric section of the T S is not for these things and that you will clearly see when you read what I have indicated to you. Persons who tell you so glibly of initiation do not know what they are talking of or else they are on the "make."

Madam Blavatsky will have nothing to do with any one who wishes to enter the section for the sake of getting powers of the magical kind and there is no way to get these except by living a pure and restrained and an ideal life.

People may tell you of other ways but I will not do you so much wrong as to give you false advice.

Yours truly,
WILLIAM Q JUDGE

Rev. W. H. Hoisington,   November 28, 1890
 Rochelle, Ill.

My dear Brother Hoisington:

I have yours asking about the book "Oahspe." This book was written by a gentleman named Broughton, in this city, who was somewhat of a medium. He was a good man but not learned in these matters, and "Oahspe" is a mass of stuff and nonsense. It is simply the result of his untrained and confused visions in the astral light, from which he has produced a medley — a sort of hash as it were — compounded of all he ever learned from the Christian Bible and what he had from other sources, as well as the wild and weird notions one can find in "The Astral Light" when he is sufficiently abnormal to see into it when he is under the influence of the effects which proceed from poor living and poor digestion. If your friend is disposed to accept this book as authority, I cannot see how I am able to counteract his belief, for the reason that a man who would accept such a jumble as this book would be likely to accept almost anything. Of course you will not tell him that. Mr. Broughton was no doubt sincere in his attempt, just as we often find many of these half-sick visionaries giving forth extraordinary ideas with sincerity.

Sincerely yours,

WILLIAM Q JUDGE

Nov 29, 1890.

My dear H. P. B.:

I have your long letter and have also read the Theosophist. Yours shows me that you feel this thing and indeed there is cause for feeling in the Theosophist than which I have never seen a more dastardly thing on the part of H. S. O. He seems to be off and is eaten up by conceit. But that is nothing new as he was always in that state and long ago I got disgusted with him and decided to let him run his affairs just as he pleased. But at the same time he has done good work for the T. S. and we must not forget this. I hope you will not let any of the fanatics in London run him down improperly. The whole situation does not depend on him altogether, and we must be generous and give him his due for the past and for the work that now does us some good. If he had not done it who would, and would those who are now made strong by the reputation of the T. S. by your work and his, have done the work themselves? Is it not a fact that they would not, but were content to wait until the matter had got into the eye of the world and been just the thing for them to take up?

He has shamefully abused you in this article and is trying to make things good for himself at your expense. All this I see and much more and while I am sorry for him, at the same time I feel as — Maharajah — feels inside that he is not the point and he is not the true difficulty. There is more and it calls for more than merely patching up a difficulty with him. If he should not resign what then? Would not the Indian work still be in the same state as before and would it not be still a grave question calling for attention? I think so. And I think that you agree with me.

I have done all I can, for I have written him not to resign but to take a rest and have further sent him the money for it. Perhaps this will make a difference when he gets it. I hope so.

I telegraphed you to wait and keep silent for the reason that the convention is so near if you take any active steps it may precipitate something bad. And I asked you also not to say anything in Lucifer for the same reason. There is no use giving that devil Harte any handle when it is not necessary. My object was for you to wait for this letter and then see what you will do.

Olcott has no power with the people who are the most important, I mean those of Europe and America. Your name is the one that is known here and in Europe and he is not known hardly. All that we have, it is recognized has come from you, our literature and all the rest. And nearly all know that Olcott never knew of the Masters and never heard from them except through you or when you were in the vicinity or through your chela Damodar. Do not therefore give him so much importance. I think you will agree that this is the best advice. After the convention has met then you will see more clearly what to do for then there will be something to go on. Just now we are in the dark unless you have some inside information.

And do not let the people in London go wild for they will sure go off the handle if they hear from you something mysterious about the future and in their mad eagerness to do what they suppose you wish they will do just what they ought not to do. I say this with all due respect for their zeal and earnestness, but at the same time I know their lack of wisdom and that they do not know yet how to wait for events.

Now to come to the point. I said that there is something more important than the question of Olcott's resignation. It is in this that India has done absolutely naught for the two great and active sections Europe and America. They must now come in irrespective of Olcott and do their part toward the second object of the T S which has been neglected by them. I propose to send out to them a circular urging that they take up this work, that a special department be made at Adyar for the benefit of the U. S. and Europe, and that the Indian members send all sorts of their stuff out of their books to us either directly or from Adyar so that we may distribute it to our members, I here and you and yours in Europe. This will tend to make India of some use, will make a strong feeling of solidarity, and after it will have the effect of getting more and more money out of America for the work and for the purpose of keeping up Adyar in good style. In short it is my idea to make India do something itself for the world and no longer lie supinely in idleness while foreigners do what the Hindus should do. Is not this a good scheme? My proposition is that the Forum be made larger so as to provide for all this matter, and that we at the different centres have the right to fix up the english and so on of all the matter and have discretion as to its publication for I know that the hindus sometimes write awful english.

Now as to carrying this out. I am, as said, disgusted with Olcott and think he is enamoured of his lectures and all that and can hardly hope to get him to do that for I have before now asked him to do it. But if he goes on a vacation it may be started. And I propose to get up a circular to the Hindus on the subject and send to them independently and ask them to meet it in their branches and have it forced on Adyar, and will offer in it to pay the cost for here, and will also send copies to India of the Forum.

This would be offering to our members a good thing and would be a practical carrying out of our second object.

Now in order to give this force I ask you to sign the enclosed so that I may print it in the circular and thus give it the weight of your name. Will you do it? Do you think it well?

I have already mentioned this plan to Bert and hope

245

he will have force to get it going, but I fear for him as he is not what is known as a bold operator. He has not enough audacity.

You can at the same time start the same thing from London and if you do you should not fail to say in it that it is done in cooperation with me so as to give it on your part what force there is from association with the American section. They may all say or think what they like but it is true that after London the next centre of activity is in this country.

I know and have for years known what is the matter with Olcott. It is this, he has never been loyal to you who gave him all he ever knew of the Masters and their wisdom. He used to say and to write the most awful mean things to me about you, and that is why I have always been disgusted with him. But I regarded him as a man whom THEY had taken to use for THEIR purposes as long as he would carry them out. I am not surprised at his attitude now for it is perfectly in line with the past and now when he has been put in the fire he shows the weakness of his disloyalty. Whatever you are and whatever faults you have in the eyes of the world I have never found you to fail about the Masters and Their wishes, and more I know that I and all the rest of the Society owe all that we prize in that line to you.

To sum up I say be quiet for a while. Wait for something to drop. Act always for the T S and if some or any of the lights of the T S go out why let them go, there is not time to stop and examine their dead bodies, we must always be up and doing something else. Please make your

246

chelas in London have some little of this spirit and let them get out of the old habit of their predecessors of going off on some personal quarrel. They always misunderstand you, right or wrong, and they have not yet learned how to find out their own strict line of duty. Do not tell them I said so as I have no wish to chide them for the reason that I am bad enough myself but to you I suppose I can sometimes talk freely.

This is all I can think of. I feel that all will be right. I have seen a vision of Adyar and I KNOW that it is a great thing — I mean Indian Headquarters no matter where it be — and no one can wipe that sight out of my memory. It may not be just now but it is potential and some day it will be evident and active.

Sincerely as ever,
WILLIAM Q JUDGE

Mr. E. W. Primm,   New York, December 1, 1890
   Belleville, Ill.
Dear Sir and Brother: —

Pray do not scruple to ask me for any services that I can render you. This office is under too great obligations to you to ever forget them. You are not the first who has asked me respecting the passage in the Countess Wacht-meister's notice in "Lucifer." The explanation is really, I think, very simple. The Countess, though a devoted Theosophist, is, like many women, not always prepared to seize the exact meaning of a proposition, and has misunderstood remarks of Mme. Blavatsky respecting the cycle. The facts are, briefly, that in the last quarter of every century special forces are put forth by the Higher Powers towards the effectuation of wholesome spiritual ends. Every Theosophical activity occurring during that epoch has the advantage of these special forces behind it, and it is for this reason that it is of so much importance for us workers to make the very most of the years left between now and 1897. At all other times, that is to say, during the other three quarters of each century, every real activity has its natural result, for spiritual agencies are not suspended during 3/4 of the time. All good work tells at any time, but at *this particular time* it has greater efficacy because of the special influences back of it.

Very sincerely and fraternally yours,

WILLIAM Q JUDGE.

Mr. Edward S. Walker,   December 4, 1890
    Boulder, Colo.
My dear Sir and Brother:

I am exceedingly glad to read your letter of the 30th ult. and also to answer it to the best of my ability, because it shows earnestness and also is quite clear. I did not intend in my last letter to intimate that you or any of your members were unfit in any way to aspire to Adeptship, but supposing from your letters that you thought Chelaship could be attained easily or by directing you to some place

248

or person, it would be well to give the warning and suggestion which I did.

The references made to the articles in the Path were in answer to that part of your former letters respecting aspiring to Chelaship, and in respect to nothing else. Any man or woman has the right to aspire and work towards Adeptship, and no person has any right to say whether they will succeed or fail. Hence it is not for me to condemn the aspiration in toto or to prognosticate the result.

I think we are now upon a proper basis to arrive at a thorough understanding, not of each other, but of Theosophy and the objects of the Theosophical Society.

In the first place the Society assumes no authority and has authorized nothing in the way of books. Mme. Blavatsky's works however are considered by the greater number of the members as good authority for them, as she appears to be the only person in these days who has been able to point out with clearness the road to be followed, either in the case of aspirants for Chelaship or by those who desire to help on the Theosophical movement. You therefore see that there are two branches to this inquiry. The first is in respect to the Theosophical movement and the second is in respect to Occultism and Chelaship, things quite different from the Theosophical movement per se.

Now first as to the Theosophical movement. That is declared to be by those who founded it an attempt to bring about a universal brotherhood, and for those who believe that there are Adepts, and that Mme. Blavatsky has correctly reported the views of the Adepts, it seems that the movement does not seek to cultivate psychical powers but to give to the world such a philosophy and ethics as shall lead to its reformation, for the world in general is in such a state as not to be fit to pursue psychical powers; and furthermore, it is quite plain in the development of the race that psychical powers are naturally coming forth, and therefore the ground in which they shall appear should be prepared beforehand with right philosophy and ethics, so that those powers shall not flourish in a "hot bed of evil passions."

Now as to the second Branch, which is the one to which your letter properly applies, the same persons hold, believing in Adepts and what is heard from them, that their views should be accepted in respect to Adeptship, Chelaship, and the like. And as the Adepts do not make themselves publicly known in the Theosophical Society, it follows that there is none in the organization which decides whether or not an applicant shall or shall not be an accepted Chela, or even a probationary Chela, or even one aspiring to probation. The Adepts through all the ages have said that "An Adept is the efflorescence of his age, the one person in the ten thousand or more who aspires to Adeptship." I would not therefore say that it is impossible for one to become an Adept in one incarnation, but all the evidences and philosophy point to the extreme difficulty of one so becoming, and to the existence of the fact that such a person has to work through many incarnations towards the end in view. Now as this is a matter connected with the inner life of each individual, it is impossible for any one to determine what is the progress or growth attained in previous incarnations or in the present;

neither can I say how is one to determine the number of his previous incarnations. But believing in evolution and the law of cycles, and reincarnation, I believe, from all that I have studied, that each one of us has been through such a number of incarnations that their extent is inconceivable; and further, I believe that if a person is very near, say one life off, to actual Adeptship, he shows it in this life in his enormous grasp of knowledge, great development of spirituality, wonderful acquaintance with natural hidden laws, and in other ways proves naturally that he is in fact ready to pass further on to Adeptship. I think this answers your question on the outside. The articles in the Path to which I referred, and also Mme. Blavatsky's book, "The Voice of the Silence," further show how this inner life of which we are speaking is a matter of great subtlety and one which cannot be subjected to the rules of any society or body of self-constituted persons, but is to be determined alone by the fraternity of Adepts, who although unseen are nevertheless great, and undoubtedly a portion of the unseen overshadowing laws of nature.

The reason why I said "the attainment of Adeptship is not the primary motive of a good Theosophist" was, that if that attainment merely be the object or motive, it will in itself frustrate the result desired, because being the primary motive it must be selfish or personal. The motive of one who wishes for Adeptship is in fact universal brotherhood and great virtue taken up after his first personal leaning has led him towards striving for Adeptship. This seems rather paradoxical, but it is true. Nature is full of paradoxes, and in these matters, while we must, in order to succeed, be thoroughly unselfish, it is yet true that no man rises to unselfishness without having first aroused the desire through selfishness. But once that he understands this he can proceed to eliminate selfish desire and endeavor to acquire the unselfish one. It is therefore true that as you say "An Adept realizes and lives up to all the highest objects of the T. S. and is the living exponent of all those best objects and aims," and I do not think I was playing upon words.

I do not wish to and did not wish to assign to you any wrong or selfish motive in a desire to attain Adeptship, but I have to sincerely state that if that desire means the desire to attain the powers of an Adept, it is a mistaken view, for the powers are merely incidentals to the *state of being* an Adept and are never desired by an Adept, notwithstanding that he may compass them, since powers are merely phenomena of inner states, just as the power to express ourselves is due to our inner mental development. Hence, the Adepts endeavor to reach a certain inner state regardless of the powers, notwithstanding that they are well aware that such and such powers come with those states. Just the same as if one desired to be a king, he would not so desire merely that he might sign warrants, letters of marque and patents and the like, which are the powers of a king, but that he should be in the kingly state, regardless of or rather inattentive, while so desiring, to what he might have to do objectively when in the kingly state.

As to telling whether or not you are sincerely energetic at working hard for the Cause of truth, that can be determined by yourself and will show itself in the outcome of your efforts. It is certainly not proper for me in advance to decide upon that question; I should be inclined to say that all persons who endeavor to organize a Theosophical Branch must necessarily have been urged thereto by some good motive.

Every one has the right to expect the Masters to help, and we think that they do help all sincere hard workers in Theosophy, who follow on the lines laid down by them; but it will be disappointing to us if we expect them *to give us evidence* that any particular Master or Masters are helping. I think the question in regard to "thought of Chelaship, why such should be yet premature" is answered by the foregoing. What I meant there was that before one proceeds to formulate such thoughts it is better to thoroughly understand about Chelaship and Adeptship.

There can be no implication, nor do I make it that you are ignorant of spiritual things or have no spiritual understanding or knowledge or may not have attained a realization of the unity of man, for those, like the others, are matters about which I have no right to decide and do not decide.

The art of applying one's theoretical knowledge follows upon the conscious possession of such knowledge. But as I have said, the knowledge about which we are speaking being about the spiritual, astral, and other unseen states of nature, it is difficult to acquire these powers and if I referred to that in my letter it was by way of caution and for no other purpose. I have no right and no desire to try to limit the aspirations of anyone.

I hope I have made this clear to you and if you desire to ask further or to have what I have said further cleared up I shall be glad to do all I can.

Fraternally yours,
WILLIAM Q JUDGE

Books to study to gain acquaintance with theosophical ideas and doctrines:

1. Key to Theosophy — H. P. B.
2. Esoteric Buddhism — Sinnett
3. Occult World — Sinnett
4. Secret Doctrine — H. P. B.
5. Bhagavad Gita — Hindu ancient book
6. Voice of the Silence — H. P. B.
7. Its Magazines — Theosophist, Lucifer, Path.

———

Franz Fullner Esq   Dec 5, 1890.
 Chicago

Dear Sir and Bro:

I have your reply to the questions and by the same mail yours to H. P. Blavatsky asking about psychic powers.

The E. S. was not established in order to train anyone in psychic development but to form an inner earnest centre for the T. S. Advanced instruction is given in it, but the universal rule in higher occultism is that generally the exhibition in oneself of psychic powers is stopped until the student thoroughly understands the philosophy and laws behind them. That is, the cultivation of those powers is not the aim of higher occultism as those powers are only phenomena which occur upon inner changes taking place. When the philosophy and laws are understood the powers may again manifest without danger. But of course there are cases where they never cease. My desire was that you should clearly understand before joining.

I therefore send the preliminary pledge for you to sign and return.

WILLIAM Q JUDGE

———

New York, 8 Dec 1890
Dear Griffiths

You ought to visit Paul Webersinn and talk kindly to him. As he has applied for and been admitted to E S I do not understand how he feels. I sent by accident a memo. from an old pad about Board of Control and may be that confused him.

Sincerely
WILLIAM Q J

Recd yours of 2^d and glad you are taking a rest. And say, they tell me I write badly but that is because they never saw your letters. Do practise a little and not write in such an awful hurry, or else have wider spaces so I can get time to decipher yours. Ha ha!

Yes go slow. We are in the middle of eternity every day and there is plenty of time. So take it easier.

As Ever
WILLIAM Q JUDGE

255

Mr. Joseph H. Fussell   December 10, 1890
    Savannah, Ga.
My dear Mr. Fussell:

I am pleased to hear from you and to know that you and Dr. Nunn have hopes of a Branch in Savannah.

The Brotherhood of Luxor to which you refer is a Brotherhood which, you might as well know now, it is impossible for any man to enter until he has passed through many lives and series of initiations, for it is in fact a Society of Adepts. I must ask you to draw a wide distinction between this Brotherhood and a fraudulent one which was started in this country, called the H. B. of L., meaning the Hermetic Brotherhood of Luxor, which was merely for the purpose of gaining money. I cannot imagine that you will find out any more than I have told you about the real Brotherhood. Neither can I condemn your desire to join it, for although you may be mistaken as to the qualifications required and the extraordinary difficulties attending entrance, your desire shows a leaning towards these matters, and for that reason I want you to bring the question up with Dr. Nunn, who is perfectly competent to explain to you the difficulties in such cases and to put you on the true basis in the beginning, so that you might avoid the long series of disappointments extending over years if you start out with the idea that such a goal could be obtained easily or without the extremest effort and study. I am,

                    Very truly yours,
                        WILLIAM Q JUDGE
                        Gen. Secretary.

Mr. A. C. Lamphere   December 15, 1890
    Jacksonville, Fla.
Dear Sir:

I have yours of the 12th in which you say "Would you kindly refer me to some advanced work on Esoteric teachings?" It must be very obvious to you at once that if there were for sale or publication an advanced work on "esoteric" teachings it would at once cease to be esoteric, since the meaning of that term is hidden or secret, notwithstanding its very loose use in America at the present time. I have been studying this subject a great many years and have yet to find any advanced publication such as you desire, for the above reason that it is an impossibility. My advice to you would be to carefully study Theosophical literature, as all through it are scattered various references and hints as to esoteric matters.

I cannot agree with you that your body or any one's body is good for a thousand years, as the human body has its limitation and cannot cohere much beyond the allotted time. I am sorry that I am not able to meet your wishes in this matter, but I am very well satisfied that experience and further study will demonstrate to you that you are asking for impossibilities. Then further it occurs to me that the true duty of man and especially a Theosophical man is not to discover any means to prolonging the miserable existence of a human body, but rather to engage in developing his inner nature, the only real one, and in helping his fellow man, in which work I would wish you all success.   Fraternally yours,

WILLIAM Q JUDGE

BLAVATSKY LONDON

IF OLCOTT RESIGNS OTHER STEPS ARE POSSIBLE THAN
BREAKING UP THE SOCIETY CABLE HIM SUGGESTING
AMERICAN OR EUROPEAN AS PRESIDENT PROCEED
SLOWLY
JUDGE

Dec 18/90

————

Miss Katherine E. Turnbull   December 18, 1890
     New York City.
My dear Miss Turnbull:
     Mr. Fullerton has handed me your remarks respecting
question 91 in the Forum, . . . and unless you will wish to
add anything further to it I will use that last page, which
amounts in fact to a new question, as to how it is possible
when the physical memory has disappeared for any one
to remember old family associations (in Devachan) and
the like. I thought the question was fully answered in
No. 91, but I see that probably Mr. Sinnett's very materi-
alistic manner of writing on these topics has made difficulties in your case. In my own studies I do not pay much
attention to his writings, excellent as they are, but content
myself with Mme. Blavatsky's. And as he got all his information from her, her statement of the philosophy is
clearer to me than his. In that it appears to be held that
Devachan is a state where the Ego enjoys and does not
suffer, suffering being reserved for the earth life. It is not

a question of memory strictly speaking, but is a state where the causes generated on this earth which can exhaust in no other state, do so exhaust themselves, leaving the causes relating to this plane of earth life to be afterwards exhausted here, and as it is, like this life, a state of illusion, the Ego naturally enlarges all its conceptions of what it thought best and highest when it was alive, for such are the causes that relate to that state.

May I ask you to be kind enough when you have read this over to send it back to me, so that I may have it by way of notes with which to formulate my answer in the Forum?

Fraternally yours,
WILLIAM Q JUDGE

———

Miss Julia S. Yates   Dec. 19, 1890
    Jamestown, N. Y.
Madame:

For your enclosure of $1.50 there will at once be mailed you a copy of "The Working Glossary" and forty copies of "Theosophy the Religion of Jesus." We do not keep in stock Dr. Anderson's "Scientific Proof of the Existence of the Soul," but order forty copies thereof to be mailed you from San Francisco. You may expect the latter in about two weeks.

The hearing of the sound to which you refer in your letter and which you have called "the occult bell," signifies, when heard by ordinary persons, a change in their physical and psychological conditions, in just the same way as a sound is heard when a glass is broken, which signifies that a glass has been smashed, that is to say, a change in condition from unsmashed glass to broken glass. It has no very great significance, and warnings are scattered all through Eastern and occult literature against attaching any significance to it further than I have stated. If one hears this sound and then imagines that it is a signal from some Adept, a mistake will be made, because an Adept would not be so wasteful of energy as to make a signal to a person who could not instantly understand from whom it was without any assistance. Such sounds are heard, as well as numerous others, by persons who indulge in training, and they always mean changes or alterations of certain unperceived conditions and centres in the body, and the warnings made against it are in order to prevent people from being led away from their true progress by giving undue attention to such phenomena.

Very truly yours,
WILLIAM Q JUDGE

———

Dear Mrs Baldwin   Dec 19, 1890
    The word is composed of three sounds
        A like Ah
        U like "u" in "true"
        M like em.
    Patanjali gives no directions for it. The tone is that

of middle "fa" and something like the wind or the waters falling.

The reference to turanian and aryan adept is not now explainable. It refers to different degrees of initiation and as we are not adepts we cannot know its real meaning.

Sincerely
WILLIAM Q JUDGE

————

New York, Dec 22 1890

Dear Griffiths

Much obliged regarding Webersinn. Tell him that his attitude is right and that although this life may be unpleasant the next one will be better. At the moment of death the whole consciousness opens and widens and we see not only the past lives but also the next new one which we have formed the causes for. I hope he may get better.

Please read enclosed from Mrs McIntire and tell me what she means from your knowledge of the facts. I just now write her and say that I do not understand and also that *we* must prepare the conditions in order that the "divine ray" may be seen.

Is she a crank or what?

Yours
WILLIAM Q JUDGE

Mr. E. F. Woodward,   Dec. 22, 1890
    Sacramento, Calif.
Dear Sir:
    I cannot expect to reply fully or authoritatively to your question as to when the Ego takes possession of the person. The subject has not been dealt with in Theosophical literature, and I suppose the reason is that it is not of very much consequence, because we know that it is a fact that the Ego does get possession of the human body. However, I doubt if such possession is obtained at birth, for children do not appear to have responsibility until somewhere about their seventh year, and such is the view intimated by Mme. Blavatsky in speaking of deaths of children before their seventh year. At birth it seems to me the human body is merely that of an animal overshadowed, so to speak, and destined to become possessed of a soul after the lapse of a few years. Consequently, all that I should be willing to say on my part would be that at birth each person has potentially a soul but not in the same sense as in the case of an adult. It does not seem to me that a question like this is one that must be classed as a necessary question to answer so as to satisfy hunger and thirst in the mind, for the reason that whichever way it is answered will make no difference, inasmuch as those who have asked the question are all adults, and children will not be at all disturbed by any such speculation as this. I have no doubt this is the reason why the matter has never been discussed, because the rules of conduct and of life are of more importance than questions of detail, such as the present question.   Sincerely yours,
    262   WILLIAM Q JUDGE

Colonel H. S. Olcott,   Dec. 23, 1890
    Adyar, Madras, India
My dear Olcott:
    At the request of Miss G. L. Leonard, F. T. S., a friend
of mine, I beg to introduce to you through this note the
Rev. Hartmann H. Russell, who goes to India as a Christian missionary to the heathen.
                        Very truly yours,
                            WILLIAM Q JUDGE

Personal

My Dear Griggs: Dec 26, 1890
    This whole Candler mess which you must admit you
have gotten up through your telling about it to the Group,
is getting disagreeable and nasty. When I first wrote
Whitaker I incautiously and inadvertently put an intended
question into direct shape of an assertion. He hotly replied
and called me a deliberate liar for which of course I do
not care a snap. And so I replied and apologized and tried
to explain. He now writes again but evidently feels as
before against me, but for that I do not care either. I am
sorry though to see him so heated and spiteful. In his letter
he refers to what he calls "unjust treatment" by H P B of
Mrs. W.—— and in this he is dead wrong, but I do not
reply to that part of his letter. He also puts a lot of cate-
gorical questions to me which he has no right to put, but
which I have answered as not caring to dispute with him.

He desired to know 1. Did I charge him with "a small part" of writing up his charge with Griggs. I answered "no." 2. Is there any reason why Griggs should not know all that I have said to Council. I ans^d "none at all." You of course shall have all the papers when they get back from California to add your own remarks. But why does W. write all this? He goes out of his way too in his letter to say H P B made the most absurd rule that was ever made in Rule 5, and cites his own experiences as a secret Society man to prove it. In fact the whole letter is full of bad feeling against me, against H P B, and against Mrs. C. What sort of a state of things is this for an E. S.? Is this ranting, fighting and criticising style of things going to do us any good? I think not my dear friend. And the whole of it is as needless. Of course I am not the judge but the tone of W's letter is a complete and violent criticism of H. P. B. It has all grown out of your telling about Mrs. C, for which you deserve a reprimand. W. visits Mrs W and his letter shows that the "facts" (?) he has from his wife prejudice him against both Mrs. C. and H. P. B.

Rule 5 *is* the most important of all, for it goes to the root of each persons personal character and vanity and I am sick to think that an old hand in T. S. like you have not shown this to W. instead of permitting yourself and him to rip ahead.

When I read his letter today I felt sick and I assure my dear friend that if I could I would cut loose from all these people, for the Boston case is only one more piled on top of a mass of instances of charges, counter charges and the like. We will not get a single word of real aid from

H P B till all this stops in every direction. And we have only 8 or 9 years left.

Well, the year 2000 may show up 5 worthy men and women in this real work, but I doubt it.

Sincerely
WILLIAM Q. JUDGE

Mrs. E. Baber-Pathorne,   Dec. 26, 1890
   Boulder, Colo.

Dear Madame:

. . . . The whole matter seems very clear from what you and Mr. Casey write. It appears to be the fact that with yourself a number of Christian Scientists applied for a Charter under some mistaken notion, which being dispelled, they see that they ought to resign. And I agree with them as long as they stand in that position. It was of course disagreeable for you to hear disparaging remarks made at the meeting, but such things occur in life and are easily forgotten and overlooked. As far as I am concerned, it is not of any moment what they say about me, especially when they wholly misunderstand my position; and in such a case it is not necessary to endeavor to dispel their illusions, when we see that it would be a difficult if not an impossible task.

I hope you have not said anything about Christian Science, or Mental Science or anything of that sort, and that if you have you will refrain carefully in the future for this reason: Theosophy can stand on its own merits and has no quarrel with any other system; consequently, the Theosophist's duty is to promulgate if he can Theosophical ideas, without disputing about the ideas of other people. When one opposes Christian Science etc. either publicly or privately, counter opposition is produced which diverts the mind from the consideration of Theosophy, but when there is no such opposition and Theosophy has a fair unimpeded hearing, it generally succeeds in gaining the day. Hence, I would suggest on your part a policy of silence as regards those doctrines in which you have no confidence, and confine yourself to explaining or bringing forward Theosophical doctrines. It is better to wait perhaps till one finds the proper material for a Branch, as the present experience abundantly demonstrates. In all probability there will be more resignations, and, if I were you, I would not oppose them nor endeavor to procure them either. If you hold before your mind what you wish to accomplish, it will be accomplished by quiet endeavor without producing opposition.

If I have not met all your queries, please let me know and I will write you further.

Regarding Branch Papers, the usual number were sent to the Secretary of the Keshava Branch, who must now have them, and if it should happen that he resigns, then the persons remaining in the Branch are entitled to the possession of them, and, if the Branch continues, succeeding Papers will be sent it in the usual course.

Very truly yours,

WILLIAM Q JUDGE

General Secretary.

My Dear Mead: New York, Dec 30, 1890

Just as I was about to write this I got the cable the last words of which are "Olcott remains," for which at this point I thank our god with a small "g".

Now please try and do this for me that I write about. I have decided not to wait for the reply to the circular to India about the papers for the Society, but have already begun. The series is to be called the Oriental Department, and will begin in Jan^y.

I have a hindu here from whom I expect to get some matter which with an article by W Q J on ethnological and phrenological studies in India will make up the first. Then I will want the second and it ought to come out in Feb sure as *I will* make this thing go or find out that it is no good. Now you and yours can get me something from London from some of the Hindus there by either making them write it themselves or by getting it in an interview and having their permission to put their name to it. Let it be on any subject. Perhaps the easiest one would be something about the religious customs of the native place of the particular hindus you ask as they all know about those. It would be interesting for the americans even if you english do not want it. I want anything in that line that I can now get hold of while I am waiting for a reply from India. Now that H S O has stayed in perhaps I can get him to help. There used to be some hindus in London who called at the rooms who can if they will say something on these

267

matters. If you are stumped then ask one of them to write me something for pay. I will pay $10 for say 1600 words. Later I will be able to regularly hire someone. Oh my dear boy those ideas are just burning me and I depend on you and the others to help me out; if you do I promise to help you and bet I can as time will show. I see a big future before us and am in a great haste not to lose a single moment. Besides H P B has given me these ideas and surely you want to carry those out, as they are not my invention. By this department I hope to enlist the fancy and the interest of men we cannot get to look at us in any other way and I "think I see" as Tom Paine said the opportunity to do it by certain channels not available to you there. If you cannot get the time then get some one who has tact and good sense to look for what I want. I know it can be got for the temporary use I have indicated above.

For instance the brahmins all are in the habit of doing certain things in the morning before eating and there is a certain way they act at meals and at funerals and at births and at deaths and christenings; also at certain days of the month they have other things they do. Also the peasants have certain ideas and thoughts about the images they set up in the fields when they are at work. All of this is unknown here and that you can get from any hindu.

Such a paper as this could be called "certain Hindu observances." That would give plenty of leeway and allow of lots of matter to come in so as to be easily written and 800 or 1600 words are not much. Another could be about the "ryots" and it could give their ideas as to idols

268

and the like. In fact let your fancy float and you will finds lots of other ways and subjects.

As to "aids and sugges." You can surely get things to answer if you will read those numbers now out as I have tried to reply to the questions and have not wholly succeeded. There several, and there are many points that you can give me your ideas on — and I mean the ideas too of all the others — such for instance as on p 9 of no 3 you will see that there are 3 basic principles given while in the Sec Doct there are 4 and the members want to know how to reconcile such things as that. You can tell them and besides a word or two now and then from London no matter who from has a good effect. Surely there is enough out already that has not been clearly answered for you to find matter still. Then again it is perfectly competent for you — I mean any one there — to say what are the details about how Kama is distributed in the body in the lifetime and what parts of us it particularly affects. That question is a practical one as it takes hold of facts that can be understood and about which the best of them are by no means clear.

For many of them do not understand, because it is so new and so opposite to modern thought, how it can be that immaterial things like the passions can take a form at any time or be more than mere effects in the astral light or other plane. Send me something on this if you like and if you will make any arrangement about it you can have matter at the same time for the E S in London, by using the same stuff before it goes to me or by having it copied.

There are such a mass of members here at distant points that something must be done about this.

As to Griggs and Whitaker I will proceed to have the thing quashed if I can but both of them are bitter and I know from some of the words in letters from Whitaker that he has listened to his wife or ex wife and thinks that she was unjustly treated in London.

Of course he had no right to talk to her about it, but such is the meaning of a pledge in these days — not worth a dmn. At the same time Griggs is bitter against Candler and he ought to get a letter from the Old Lady setting him down and not in the usual style that only makes him feel to be a great man and one who merely gives in at the request of an old friend. The E S is full of this kind of thing.

In Iowa there is the woman I wrote of last and in other places others. If there was a grand pan out there would be few indeed who could remain. Then you speak of certain persons not qualifying for the Inner. How can they do this when the notice says that they must not ask about it.

As ever yours

WILLIAM Q. JUDGE

Dec 30, 1890.

Dear Arthur

Just now I got a Cable from H P B. it reads:

"Stop Griggs and Whitaker now for lamb's sake. Olcott remains."

Last words refer to H S O's proposed retirement from the presidency. Can't you get Willard to have this fact printed? He can say that the Convention met and Olcott asked leave to retire for health and instead takes a vacation and does not retire.

The first part refers to Candler matter.

Now "Sir Griggs" let us see that '91 starts in with hatchets buried. The Old Lady has enough on her back. Her body near died the other night when she left it to go to India to work on Olcott. Do not burden her with any troubles. Tell Whitaker something. Get him to withdraw charges. Tell him you acted hastily before you heard from H P B as she had the matter from me and that you thought I intended not to tell her. Anything at all. Get the thing done before '91 sets in. There is greater work to do than fighting haystacks. I have apologized to Whitaker for an offense I never committed. Pacify. He said in his last that his wife was unjustly treated in London. This is the key. He is down on Candler perhaps for that though she had nought to do with it. Mrs. W. was cited before the whole council and refused before her Higher Self to stop her dealings with sexual and astral spooks and was disappointed because she was not regarded as anything more than a mere hysteriac. But don't tell W. this.

271

Much depends now on each unit and let us start in fresh and smiling with personality out of sight for 1891.

Now do please attend to this. As you and W are brothers ∴ or ☐ you ought to be able to fix it up; and I will tear up the stuff when it gets back from the West.

As Ever Yours

WILLIAM Q. JUDGE.

——————— 1891 ———————

Mrs. Baber Pathorne   Jany 6 1891
Dear Madame

    Real Concentration is in fact Union with the Divine.
We are to understand that we are each the Divine. There
is no separateness but the one Spirit is in each reflected in
each person. This truth, expressed by the ancients as
"Thou art that spirit" is to be well understood and felt before concentration can become possible. Ordinary concentration of attention is merely an outward show but of
course necessary also in the real concentration. Now
having deeply thought over this you should study such a
book as Patanjali's yoga Philosophy, which is the philosophy of concentration and in which you should find much
light on this topic. The true source for concentration is
selflessness, for as long as we feel the shackles of the personal self, so long is concentration hindered in various
ways. I think in the above is what you need if you will
study it out for it needs much thought.

Sincerely
WILLIAM Q JUDGE

———

Mr. Theo. G. E. Wolleb,   Jan. 6, 1891
    East Oakland, Calif.
Dear Sir and Brother:

    I have yours of the 24th. I received your expression of
sympathy, but the fact that I did not answer it should not
make you suppose that I did not care for it. I have so

275

many letters to write that it did not seem necessary to acknowledge this kindness in the pressure of business. I am very glad that the photograph struck you as it did, and only hope that it may really express what the person is. I think you are quite right in acquainting yourself with all that you can; such an acquaintance of course does not assume that you wish to attempt practice, but at the same time it is utterly impossible to know how a sound is made in a "proper way" unless one tries it. This sound is a different thing from ordinary book learning. I hope my answer did you service. As to the words "vile moral passion" we must always make allowances for Mme. Blavatsky's nationality and modes of expression, as she does not claim to be a professor.

Affinity and gravitation should not be mentioned in the list you quote because they are results or aspects of such things as cohesion, electricity, and magnetism; hence, as to that, there is no inaccuracy. There is of course a correspondence between all these saktis and sons of Fohat; but we are not enough advanced to really understand them; book learning is not enough. This is why we cannot fully grasp what H. P. B. says and often misunderstand her. Everything should not be accepted as Gospel. She wishes us to use our intelligence and judgment. If we did follow H. P. B. "as our sun" we should do well. The trouble is that we gauge her by our own small natures and thus think the example is not good. I hope some day to be out your way.

Sincerely yours,
WILLIAM Q JUDGE

Dear Bro Blodgett   Jan 12 1891

I have yours and glad to see that you can give $50. a month for 3 months. Will you therefore kindly send me the $50. for January? May I ask you to send that for Feby on the 1st. Funds are low and I am not able just now to advance to the Gen Sec'y funds.

As to business and retirement. My view is that a man should always face his Karma which is then of use to him but if shirked it is not useful. If one is in a business not liked and can get no other, by sticking to it and acquiring the ability to be *in* it but not *of* it then great good results. Under the facts you give I should say to remain in business for the present for as you say the T. S. is poor and needs funds. It was by remaining steadily in business that I have been able to keep up the Path and other matters when there helpers were few; and I still stick to it. One needs a counterbalance and business gives it; and it also gives to the T. S. the strength derived from the very fact that its members continue to do all their duties.

Like you I see no reward here worth getting. There is no reward and no permanence nor real happiness except in the life of the Spirit, and that is not gained by running away from Karma. As Bhagavad Gita says, "there is no world up to Brahma's that is free from Karma." Hence we do not escape it but only change one sort for another when we "kick against the pricks" and seek for new environment.

Ever Sincerely
WILLIAM Q JUDGE

My Dear Mrs Stubbs:

The words "spirit" and "spirituality" have probably been used by you in your thoughts, to mean only the *good* that is in the world and in man, whereas they have another meaning. Spirit is the active pole or end of that *one thing* which has at its other end or pole, matter. Hence spirit is life and activity and as there is both good and bad activity and life, it follows that we may say "spiritually good, or bad." Spiritually good is the highest sort of good and spiritually evil is the highest, most subtle, and unseen kind of evil. So a black magician is one who does his acts and thoughts on a plane of life not seen by us and which is therefore, as far as we are concerned, spiritual. If you do not call it "spiritual evil" you will have no word with which to name it and therefore will lose an idea and that is impossible. You cannot call it "materially evil" for that means quite another thing, that is evil as related to the objective world, and thus in that case the whole unseen world is left out of sight, which is incorrect in a philosophical sense. — Nirmanakaya means one who has the power to live in the sphere of the world in an invisible body in which he has all his powers as if he were not dead. Now a powerfully bad man can accomplish this, but at the same time it is better only to think of good Nirmanakayas.

Sincerely yours,

WILLIAM Q. JUDGE.

Dear Griffiths   New York, Jan 28 1891

Yours with Dr Cook and Mrs Thomas pledge recd.

As to privacy of papers. I have done all I could and surely the rules are definite enough. I refer to it in the next Aids. It is useless to nag at them continually and the reckless inattention prevalent everywhere is enough to make a darkey smile at the idea of such people even knowing anything. This is why H. P. B. will not give out real "pucka pucka" secrets. They are not safe. They are all probationers, and even among themselves indulge in constant gossip and irrelevancy. The process of trying them has to go on slowly and some will emerge. We can remind them now and then. But as they are constantly breaking *all* the Rules it is useless to pick out one sort of infraction. What they do succeed in learning will be just that much gained anyway in this life. They are all, so to say, children whom we are trying to show how to deport themselves before they go to higher branches. Meanwhile, they are so ignorant they suppose they are all incipient adepts. Of course there are several notable exceptions and these latter save the necks of the rest.

As Ever

WILLIAM Q JUDGE

Jan 29, 1891

Dear Mrs Wyman

Enclosed are 6 copies Order of Ins. for your E S.

Modern astrology is more or less wrong, but if the times are *accurately known* to the minute of birth the ruling planet may be found. But, we may be the rulers of the stars instead of they ours. The rising star and house is the ruler, but the moon and sun may be either the hyleg or body ruler.

Sincerely

WILLIAM Q JUDGE

————

N Y Feb 5, 1891.

Dear Mead:

Now for yours of the 24th, the long one the longest. I am not mad nor shall I be. You must remember that my words do not represent me. Brahmins article: with the paper the letter said it was to go in Lucifer, but I would not use it anyway.

Re Griggs. Please remember that this is all fixed up except for H P B and she had best ignore it. Griggs was down here and he is trying to settle with Whitaker. So merely pass it into the hole.

Sherburne. First you say in this letter "S is expelled" and then "S has done nothing and is not expelled" which is it. In fact you have four or five sorts of things in the letter about Gahan, Murray and Sherburne and I must ask you to send me just the record whether expelled or suspended or what in each case and give no reasons. Your letter is mixed and I cannot unravel. Three lines will do, just take the said names and opposite write their status. I have Gahan suspended and Murray also and nothing about Sherburne.

As to Bert. I never notified the council as I consider all very leaky and so I will say nothing. It is none of their affair.

Re Dvivedi's book. My boy you have not read the book right; you have read the notes only I'll bet a hat and the notes are not the book by a long shot. Kindly read the APHORISMS and tell me if you ever saw such chocktaw. I never did in my life. And it was to those I referred and not the notes. The latter are good but they are not the book. No sane man in reading those aphorisms could make anything of them. I admire the notes but what the devil kind of a translation that makes rot of the text and then puts in good notes. Wait till I have a chance to show you just four feet distant and you will see. But really I would ask you to tell me candidly if you have taken any three aphorisms of the two editions and compared them and if so do you say still that he has made any sense of them. What is a translator for anyhow? I never said Dvivedi was "a damn fool." I think him a learned man and all his own writing shows that but he has made a mess of these aphorisms.

Re Charters. I must ask you for a formal letter, short, saying the charters are all recalled for the purpose of sending out others.

Re Olcott. I now get the mail from India very quickly and have the whole thing in my possession. Of course the proposal by H S O to modify the pledge is folly, but at the same time I would not give such heed to these things they will come to nothing, and I do not think it will be wise to act to O as if he were all in the wrong. Treat him nicely and do not let him see that you suspect him of anything, and do not keep the idea that if he came to London he would make trouble. That does not follow at all. H P B can deal with him alone. In the past I have seen many troubles arise from noses going in where they do not really belong, and if I were you I would only say just what I had to say by force as it were and let all things work themselves right.

You err in supposing that I think anything about H P B and what she does. All she does goes and I dont think of anything but what I have to do myself as that is all I can swing. The whole event has come out right and as I said long ago there was no need of a lot of plans about various contingencies. For the moment the American idea has won and that is enough. We have a year to work in and if it is spent well then the next one will be all right.

I'll tell you why some here are disgusted with the methods of some in London — not you. We write letters about business and go to a lot of trouble and so many errors are made and so many letters not attended to and the like we feel like laughing all the time and give it up. The mutual letter business between London and N Y was tried *several* times and we did as we said we would but the other side did not, and as it is some trouble to get a competent man to agree to do the work on the promise that he will get the

282

matter from London he is naturally disgusted when he does not get it. In my own case I started once and the first thing I got was a long disquisition on theosophy in general which I can write here and didnt get a word of news. So my boy I have given it up and will trust to luck and the prophet mohamet for the future. It is all right, I can swim anyhow and anywhere and if I get things all right, and if I dont why Ill make them for myself out of the filmy web of space and find they go as well as the rest. It would be better though if there was some systematic way of getting the news for the month in regular order and before the issue of the mags.

I have asked for the sake of the lord if Annie Besant cannot come to our next convention, if we pay, and I hope she will. She can make some money here as she has been much talked of in the papers and she could lecture and the halls would be crowded all the time.

Please do not forget to see that H P B writes a good letter in the beginning of March for the April convention here. We think it will be held at Boston as we have had enough of Chicago.

Dont forget this. I am awfully obliged you took so much trouble to write and especially on the night of the lecture which I wish I had heard. Do not overwork yourself.

Some steps must be taken to get Fawcett out of the Adyar place as he is in fact an enemy but after all perhaps he will put himself out. How nicely Harte has been left out of the convention report and how all his fine schemes fell to pieces. But we must only laugh and not exult for

283

to tell the truth he is a weak man who can hardly be blamed.

Letters are a nuisance and I must try to get over and hob nob with you. I would pay high to be able to go there in one day and not have to waste so much time in journeying.

Adieu and love to all and may you be blessed.

WILLIAM Q. JUDGE.

Feb. 5, 1891

Dear Mrs. Langford:

Enclosed is your receipt for dues as F. T. S. at large. The T. S. is prospering. The story about Olcott is untrue. He, being sick, has been given a leave of absence with Keightley in charge at India. Olcott goes perhaps to Melbourne. We have furnished the cash for his trip. These base lies that go about are not all due to newspapers but are furnished in part by those who ought to know better but whose bile and spite make them violate the commands of the gentle Jesus whom they pretend to follow.

Sincerely

WILLIAM Q JUDGE

Many thanks for ticket.

Mrs. A. N. Savery,   February 5, 1891
    New York City
Dear Mrs. Savery:

Replying to your letter just received about Colonel Olcott, I must ask you to disperse a few misunderstandings which I will mention in order.

1. That the Adepts — called sometimes the Masters — ever accomplish ordinary results by the use of extraordinary means. It would be an extraordinary means to adopt that of giving a large sum of money procured by the use of magic power for the purpose of carrying out the objects of the T. S., or for the purpose of aiding any of its workers in their usual and bounden duty. But They have always and still continue to impress those of us who have the means or the power to not only work ourselves but to help the rest who are working. And by means of such impressions and impulses the money was three months ago furnished and sent to India, in advance and without knowing that it would be needed for the very purpose to which it is now being applied, that is, the initial expenses of Olcott's trip.

2. That the American Branches and members are being asked alone to contribute to his expenses. The Indian Branches are being asked and are about to contribute, not only to that but also to the Society's work.

3. "That Olcott and H. P. B. went to India because the latter was supposed to be the place where alone the true doctrine was to be found." That was not the reason. They went to India for the reason that it is a centre for

work where there are stores of ancient learning and ethics valuable for every country.

4. That the Indian Section has means. The fact is that it is very poor, far poorer than the American Section, for the reason that the rich Indians are not so numerous as is supposed and a great many of them are not members.

It is a wholly wrong view to take of the Masters that their efforts are to be gauged by the amount of money which they furnish. If they do furnish any money whatever, directly, it is to persons who never reveal that fact.

These things have been explained over and over again in the only public manner accessible to us, that is to say, in addresses before our Branches and in my publications. It is also fully explained and dwelt upon in many Theosophical books and printed documents. The sooner that all of us get rid of the idea that help from the Masters means money the better for us. It is my belief that they do not furnish money, and furthermore, I have seen it proved in fifteen years that if we had a lot of money in hand before people were ready to be benefitted by its use, it would have been an injury rather than the opposite. Now, however, the seed having been sown, it is time for us who have energy and means to apply them in whatever way we can do the most good, for none of us are any more than trustees for the money and the energy we may have in our possession.

Very sincerely yours,

WILLIAM Q JUDGE.

Mr. Joseph H. Fussell,　　　　　　February 18, 1891
　Savannah, Ga.
Dear Sir and Brother:
　I have your letter of the 14th in which the principal
questions to be answered are
　1st In respect to Reincarnation and the apparent contradiction between "Isis Unveiled" and later declarations
by Mme. Blavatsky, and
　2nd In respect to the use of the term "A personal
God."
　The first question to which you refer has been fully
answered by Mme. Blavatsky herself in the Path in 1886
and '87. The articles are headed "Theories About Reincarnation and Spirits," and the first one is in the Path of
November '86 and the second of January 1887. There is
in fact no contradiction for the statement you quote from
volume I of "Isis" is correct, and neither it nor the subsequent explanations conflict with the "Key to Theosophy,"
page 134 and 140, for in the latter a clear distinction is
made between the Skandhas of — that is that belonged
to — a certain being — that is to say to the person or Ego
who reincarnates. Writing in 1875 without any nomen-
clature in general use, Mme Blavatsky used the term
"Astral Monad," which in connection with the term "individual" shows that she was speaking of the personality
which it is known is contained in the Astral soul or Astral
body, and this latter dissipates after death. Consequently
there could be no reincarnation as a rule of the same individual. The reincarnation is the reincarnation of the
Ego, which is much higher than the personality or Astral

person. I think by reading the articles referred to in connection with what you have quoted you will clear this up.

The second question about "A personal God" is really one of terms. It does not seem to me to make any difference whether you mean your personal God or my personal God, for if you have an idea of a God, then you make a being who is separate from yourself and from me, and in that sense the word "personal" has been used and in some cases the word anthropomorphic. Mme. Blavatsky does not believe in postulating the existence of God as separate from any thing, person or object in the universe; that is to say, God is everything; consequently we are unable to say who or what is God. There is a difficulty in the use of these terms, but as I understand it the words "personal God" always are understood to mean an extra cosmic being or a being who is distinct and separate from all others.

I do not know now where you can find the full explanation of the 12 Nidanas and 4 truths. Nidana means a center of energy or the beginning of a cause, and I think the four truths to which you refer are the four truths of Buddhism. But the secrecy mentioned on page 45 I think only refers to the teaching relating to the other truths above the four truths which had been revealed. The 12 Nidanas are terms used in some of the Indian schools. I will look the matter up a little more carefully.

I saw the article in the "Arena" to which you refer, and thought it interesting, and I also read the quotations to which you referred from Max Muller.

Referring again to the "Personal God" question, I think

that there *is* a flavor of personality or rather of separation in the quotation from the 4th chapter of John, because you see that it says "He is a spirit," and as I think if there be a God such as you refer to he must also be matter, then the God referred to in John is not the one including matter. I do not think that Jesus spoke of the Absolute or of the very Highest when he said, "My Father and My God," but referred to His Higher Self alone.

Sincerely yours,

WILLIAM Q JUDGE

Franz Fullner, Esq.   Feb 19th 1891
Dear Sir and Brother:

In reply to yours of the 17th inst.

1. The trance state is not "a faithful state," (i.e. not to be relied upon) except in the case of high initiates.

2. The Masters do not generally give information through such a state, and only to very advanced persons.

Fraternally yours,

WILLIAM Q JUDGE

P. S. I do not know the meaning of your sentence: "is it not a grief and a snare to me as a listener to such things?" But trances are nearly always illusions and not to be depended upon. Our duty is to try to acquire spiritual and not astral insight. Trances are nearly always on the astral plane of Nature.

289

Feb 19, 1891

Dear Gahan:

Rec^d prel. Memo. and also $6.00. Thanks.

I send this care of Wing. Hope you will come out all right. Be careful and *think* before you act and dont *always* act.

All other papers are in my possession.

All well

As ever

WILLIAM Q JUDGE

———

Mrs. Helen E. L. Fenton,   February 20, 1891

Jamestown, N. Y.

Dear Madame:

Replying to your questions of February 17th. The subject of concentration and its culture was well dealt with in the Path, Vol. 3, on page 116, and Vol. 4 on page 329, and I would recommend that those articles be studied with care, as they were meant so to be used.

Real concentration is not acquired by experiments in thought transference, but in those one of the persons has to be passive or over sensitive. Passivity leads at last either to indifference or to undue and unequal development of psychism, which is very undesirable. This is not in my opinion the road to true concentration.

There are two kinds of concentration. First, that of the mere brain and nerves, including attention, and Second, that sort which is higher and spiritual, pertaining to the ideals of life and the soul itself. The first is properly cultivated by ordinary methods of study and attention, especially the latter and which results in good memory. The second is cultivated by fixing the aspirations on the highest good for all and on the unity of all beings; by acting for the good of all; by practising altruism; by endeavoring to spread the light of truth to as many persons as possible, ignoring what seems like present advantage to oneself; in fact, by "right speech, right thought, and right action." All this second practise results in giving to all the qualities in the being, to every cell and atom, one single impulse and direction; and when that is fully established knowledge flows in on all sides as it were spontaneously. Any other practise may delude us by seeming agreeable or fascinating, but in fact results only in small special effects.

There is a point beyond which these practises of thought transference, psychometry and what not can never go. It is soon reached, and their complete ignorance of what follows is the result, together with the possibility of a negative or passive state of mind being acquired. It really amounts to nothing in the end, because we die soon and all such outer effects and acquirements die with us. Only our real inner character remains and that is improved or enlarged only by a spiritualized life and motive. That is to say, for example, take two persons, one of whom solely practised for these apparent outside effects and acquirements, and the other wholly ignoring them spent life in trying to understand the doctrine, the ethics of Theosophy, promulgating them clearly to all.

The first person really accomplished nothing, while the second has cleared away much rubbish from his character, has established himself firmly, has acquired much good helpful karma and will emerge in the next life vastly higher than the first, and in a position to intelligently take up and understand all those laws and forces which will give greater power to aid and benefit the race.

This is my firm conviction and the experience of those whom I revere. Will you read this to your fellow members?

Fraternally,

WILLIAM Q JUDGE
General Secretary.

———

Dear H. P. B.:   New York, Feb. 20, 1891

ABOUT CHANGING THE NAME OF THE E. S. — IMPORTANT.

I telegraphed to wait three days for this proposed change and again that "new name is the same as the one of Butler." This means that the name "Esoteric School of Theosophy," is precisely the title adopted by the infamous Hiram Butler affair for their school in which they had and have pupils, and get and get money in it for the rot they give out. They are not out of existence, as Butler when hunted out of Boston went to California and there has more followers and carries on his trade in the same way. It seems to me that to adopt his name is the very worst possible fate that could come to the E. S. Besides

292

I cannot see the necessity for any change of name. If it is from a desire to cut the E S off from the T S that will not accomplish the end, for the reason that you can never do so, as every one still will think it a part of the inside work of the T S as long as you are alive and stay in the Society. And why there should be any wish or desire to cut the E S off from the T S, I cannot see, and as all members of the E S have first to be F T S it cannot be done without a complete and unnecessary back down. For another reason also and that is, that you have distinctly shown over and over again that the object of the E S is to strengthen and support the T S, and as a fact it has already done so and has been of the very greatest benefit to the Society. Why then should any unnecessary distrust be created by altering the name?

Furthermore, not only has Butler used the new name, which I see has been already set up in the Press in London, but others of less fame and infamy have also, and there are several who pretend to give the same under the same name. It would be the very wildest break for us to do this after living so long with a name that is in fact protected by its intimacy with the name of the T S. May I not, from my knowledge of the whole society here, ask you to not make this change.

I would like also to call attention to the mass of stuff in the way of pretty but useless decorations put on the matter which has just been gotten out on the press. It is a jumble of everything, from gods acting as mortals to assortments of snakes out of place, and used with other symbols with which they never had any unity or corre-

spondence. Is it not, and has it not always been a grievous thing to mix the symbols? And are they not all mixed
up on this new title page? There is the two pillared hall,
and then a style of pillar that has nothing to do with that
hall; and then snakes who never appeared in that hall by
any chance for they belonged to another degree; then
there is the winged globe which truly belongs to the two
pillared hall but not in the form taken in your seal which
is for another purpose, and represents a different thing;
then there is the hindu symbol with the sanskrit letters
in the centre — this certainly has nothing to do with the
two pillared hall; then, and least of all, there is on the
top a whole line of snakes with balls on head across the
top, and they were never used in a mere apprentice
degree: other sorts of snakes and other objects have place
there. In fact it is all mixed up, and, while very well
drawn, has no place whatever in the E S at this time,
judging from what I have learned. I make bold to give
these views because I am sure you in person did not
make these up for use, but that some one else has made
them who has not a real acquaintance with the use and
meaning of the symbols.

Finally, if the name is changed — there is quite likely
to be aroused a feeling of distrust among those who as
yet do not know reasons and are not able to guess them,
and if it be said to them that the reason is so as to cut
it off from the T S then it is very natural to ask: why was
this not done in the beginning and provided for? ?

Referring again to the pictures. Look at the initial
word and say if anyone ever heard of a god representing

294

reincarnation dressed as one and, being osirified, has the right to the crown of both upper and lower Egypt? It does not represent silence at all — it attempts to show reincarnation but fails of its object. My practical opinion is that for the present section of the E S the less there is of these ornaments and symbols the better and the more unmixed the effect on the members.

As Ever

WILLIAM Q JUDGE

W. P. Phelon, M.D.   February, 1891

Sudden efforts to avert danger not preceded by a course of preparation are not of much use. The old maxim "in time of peace prepare for war" applies here and means that members should be so taught and prepared that they would not be disturbed. I do not think Street has anything behind him but native shrewdness — As I do not know just in what way members are being attacked or in difficulty I am at loss as to advice except as just said above.

[W. Q. J.]

C. H. Little Esq.   Mar 2, 1891
      Freeport Ill.
Dear Sir and Bro:

Respecting *Karma* and *action*. Karma means *action* in Sanscrit and covers *all* action. Hence it is the universal action in any manvantara thus, including all human action as well as that which is only cosmic. If we became Karmaless of course neither action nor its fruit has any effect on us. In order to become that we must be free from any effect upon us of the result or fruit of action. As all act is the mere outward expression of a thought it follows that thought is at the root of all action. And our thought is fixed always upon results or fruits and not so much on the act itself. If one can conscientiously do right acts solely because [line missing] is wholly unattached by the result or by desire for result then there is no Karma for that person. Karma attaches through one personal thought at the root of the act.

You are quite right in saying that the phrase *our* or *my* Karma is philosophically incorrect. We can have no Karma distinct from others. But we are obliged to use these words so as to express ourselves since, not seeing all the connections of Karma we appear as if having a Karma of our own. And indeed in one sense we have such Karma because otherwise it would never react upon any special individual as we know it does.

                              Sincerely
                          WILLIAM Q JUDGE

G. H. Baldwin, Esq   Mar 2, 1891
Dear Bro Baldwin:

I am sorry to have to write you this letter. But in conversing today with Bro Fullerton he dropped some remarks which led me to put questions to him and then discovered that you had spoken as follows:

(1) Told him you were in the E. S., although you have no proof that he is in it nor asked for any.

(2) Told him the names of several members of the E. S. in Washington;

(3) Told him that you had had an E. S. group there but it was now dissolved;

(4) Told him that you had spoken to Mrs Scooles in Trenton and asked her to join the E S.

(5) Told him that Bro Savage drinks too much wine.

Now my dear Bro Baldwin if rules and pledges mean anything they are to be observed; and the rules are distinctly against all the above. And even if there were no rules all this would be very improper in an E. S. member. You do not yet possess proof that Bro. Fullerton is in the E. S. and yet you discussed these things with him without requiring proof of membership. The fact that he is in my office is no proof of this.

Why was it needful to circulate about Bro Savage who is doing his best for B. T. S. a rumor affecting his character and standing? Is not the very genius of the E. S. against this last?

I write to call your attention to what is a serious matter and not to scold for I shall not speak to anyone else. But surely first the rules are to be observed, and second an E. S.

member should be the last one to unnecessarily circulate damage rumors about a fellow F. T. S.

This occurrence is no [line missing] would go far toward my advising the Head of the Section not to permit a Group in Washington as the rule of its secresy would not be observed if members violate lesser rules as shown above. Bro. Fullerton knows nothing of this letter at all and has had no part in it.

Sincerely and fraternally,
WILLIAM Q JUDGE
Sec to H P B

———

Mar 12, 1891

Dear Miss Turnbull:

I beg to acknowledge yours returning the E. S. papers. It is probably best for you to wait for the present. As some of the papers say, "one should consider long before giving a pledge, but having given it it should be kept rather than life itself." Now altho' the pledge seems to leave to our judgment obedience to leaders it is impossible to go under a leader through whom one pledges to one's Higher Self and except the leader from the pledge. For there being but *one* Higher Self and not several, the pledge thus made is to those who lead the Section as well as to Those behind it. This real distinction — or rather synthesis — is seldom observed, even when stated, but still exists. I know there are many things alleged against H P B, and also know of my personal knowledge of the

298

falsity of 3/4 of them, and it is not well for one to join the E. S. even with the reservation in the pledge, until full confidence exists. Outside of the E. S. one can progress for that body has no monopoly of truth, seeking now just to cohere and strengthen the T. S. and to perhaps enlighten those few who are sincere and devoted.

Fraternally
WILLIAM Q JUDGE

P. S. Regarding this in yours: ". . . that so baneful an element as that of personal authority should manifest itself in any modern presentment of universal truths etc." It must be remembered that the E. S. is *not* the T. S., but is a special body with its own rules. It is not for universal use and what inner knowledge it may give is not for universal promulgation. The T. S. is the body which is to make the "presentment" you speak of, and hence the "regrettable" thing — truly so indeed — is not to be in any sense predicated of the E. S. If this personal authority entered into the T. S. then of course you would be quite right. But it does not; and no one has been so clear and persistent in decrying personal authority as H. P. B. has. That is why she printed Patterson's letter in Lucifer as against Mrs. Besant's.

There have always been and will be forever the exoteric and the esoteric bodies. The first heterogeneous, the second homogeneous. And no esoteric body could be useful unless united in all parts. So it has been that altho the E. S. was begun in 1875 it consisted for years of but 7 or 8 members in U. S.

Mrs. Annie Besant,   March 13, 1891
   19 Avenue Road,
     Regent's Park, London N.W., England
Dear Mrs. Besant:

Herewith I beg to send you a draft on Smith, Payne, and Smith, London, for £20-9-5, the equivalent of $100, as an advance toward the expense of your steamer passage to New York. I have not been able yet to finish all arrangements about your lectures, but generally what I propose is that you should lecture in any event in New York and Boston, and if other places offer, when or before you arrive, at those also. . . .

If you arrive on the 8th, as is expected of the steamer, City of New York, you will have the whole night of the 8th, all day and night of the 9th, and all the morning of the 10th to rest. The hall I propose to take in New York, which is the only one available in consequence of the short notice, is Masonic Temple Hall, which seats a thousand people; the hall in Boston is the Tremont Temple, a very large and splendid hall with a fine organ in it. The distance in time between New York and Boston is six hours, the mileage being 250, and express trains running morning, middle of the day, two in the evening and at night. I have no doubt that we will succeed in getting back all the expenses. Your telegram reading "60 pounds" I construed to mean exclusive of the steamer fare, and consequently added to it forty pounds more.

Another thing that has occurred is this: In consequence of some letters of mine published in the Washington papers replying to lectures by a prominent Catholic pro-

300

fessor upon Theosophy, quite an excitement has been raised there, and the President of the Spiritualist Society there offered to the President of the Theosophical Society in Washington that they would pay for a hall if you and I would go down to Washington and publicly debate with this professor, the Spiritualists promising to back us up, and no doubt the latter would come to the debate. I replied that until I heard from you I could not debate, so that the matter stands in that state. I am also trying to make an arrangement with some Brooklyn women about a lecture before them in aid of Anna Dickenson, about which I wrote you, but as yet have nothing definite. Hoping that you will receive this money all safely and that we shall soon see you here in good health, I am

Sincerely yours,

WILLIAM Q JUDGE

PS. Please do not omit to send me materials for a sketch of your life. I hope it has been sent as I shall need it before I can have your reply to this.   J

Dear Miss Harte   Mar 16, 1891

I am so very very busy with Mrs Besant's tour and such things that for some weeks I cannot give proper legal advice. I should now advise you to see your own lawyer upon such matters so that they can have proper attention.

Otherwise you can ask me for advice. And I think

patience is what you need. Life is full of trouble always but that is lessened if we accept it and rise above it. The members of your group will no doubt give you all needed encouragement also. All proper questions in T. S. studies I will answer, cheerfully. But just now in legal matters I would be of no use as I will not be able to give them the mental attention which all such need as I know from experience.

Sincerely
WILLIAM Q JUDGE

Mrs. Annie Besant,   March 17, 1891
   19 Avenue Road, Regent's Park,
     London N.W., England
Dear Mrs. Besant:

It is of great importance to me to know how much time you will be able to pass in this country after Convention and it would be a great convenience to me if you could telegraph me thereof. A very simple telegram will suffice: for instance, if you can stay two weeks the mere words "two weeks" will be comprehensible. I need this because of possible arrangements for lectures in Springfield and other points.

It is the judgment of the Boston Branch that it would be better for the arrangement I last gave you to be changed, and that you should not lecture in Boston prior to the Convention, but devote your time to this neighborhood. It is also thought that the first lecture in Boston should be "The Message of Theosophy to the Western World," and the second, "London, its Wealth and its Poverty," the third, "Dangers" or "English Freethought." I venture to make a suggestion on a somewhat collateral matter. My first idea had been to invite the attention of socialists and nationalists to your projected visit, in order to interest all classes naturally in sympathy with your career, but I have been rather inclined more lately to think that it would be prudent if you abstained from any close connection with the socialistic party in this country. I do not refer at all to the merit or demerit of their views, but simply to the fact that in this country socialism is fully identified with anarchistic ideas and practises, this being especially the case in Chicago in consequence of the dreadful riots and murders which took place there several years ago. In view of the local feeling in America, I think that your influence as either a social reformer or a Theosophical speaker would be impaired if it was supposed that you represented a class of opinions believed by the community to be identical with those of the Chicago anarchists. No doubt you will take this suggestion into consideration. As you will still have time to write me before the sailing of your steamer, I would especially like to ask which, in your judgment, are the best of your lectures.

I have had very serious difficulty in respect to the engagement of a hall, nearly everything here at this season being taken, and the time being so short, in consequence of which all halls nearly were engaged. I have almost decided to take Scottish Rite Hall 29th St and Madison Ave and have first lecture on 13th on Theosophy and its Message to West. World and on the 15th and 17th of April also at same place.

I would also ask you to try and get an interview in London before you start so that it may be cabled here. I think if you send a note to Arthur Warren London correspondent of the Boston Herald telling him of your projected trip he will probably use it and may interview you. If that fails you, you can try and find the London office of N Y Herald and they will do it. They have a London edition. All you have to do is to send them word giving facts and your address so they can see you if they wish.

If you know Capt Bowers of Boston a leader in the Nationalist movement you can get him to handle the Arthur Warren business for you as he is personal friend of the latter gentleman, and is still in London.

Sincerely and in haste

WILLIAM Q JUDGE

————

Geo. F. Moore Esq   Apl 3, 1891
    Montgomery, Ala
Dear Bro Moore:

The rules require that the papers should be returned to me if not used. If at any other time you wish to consider them you can have them.

The other societies permitted to a member are:

304

Free Mason, Odd Fellows, and the various labor and insurance societies. The prohibition is against Societies for Occultism. The matter seems easy to decide. If you are in some other Society for Occultism then of course you cannot enter E. S.

Sincerely

WILLIAM Q JUDGE

———

Mr. Pehr LeMander   April 17, 1891
    Roslindale, Mass.
My dear Friend:

. . . . The pictures which have come are excellent as far as Subba Row is concerned, and I hope the next one of Subba Row will be equally good. My picture is a little dark, I think, as you made my eyes black, whereas they are gray, and my beard black, whereas it is brown. Please note that Subba Row's nose was not flat at all, and in your next picture, if you are able, you may make a suggestion showing that his nose projects as well as being wide. Still, I think the one that I have here is excellent in every respect, and if you are in the slightest doubt at all about it, just make the next one precisely similar to this. Please let me know definitely about the charges as others are asking now.

Yours truly,

WILLIAM Q JUDGE

To the Editor of ——   May 9th 1891

So many rumors and statements have appeared in the New York papers to the effect that Madame H. P. Blavatsky died three weeks ago and that the death was concealed until yesterday, I beg to say that a cable just received by me from the private Secretary of Madame Blavatsky states as follows: — "She died Friday the eighth of May at Two Twenty-five in the afternoon. Mead."

This hour in London would be about nine A. M. here, and the telegram of announcement to me was received here between one and two P. M.

Yours truly,

WILLIAM Q JUDGE
General Secretary

E. S. T. S.

AMERICAN DIVISION.

NEW YORK (P. O. Box 2659), *May 9, 1891.*

TO THE MEMBERS OF THE SECTION.

Group Presidents will send a copy hereof to all their members at once.

Notice is hereby given that the undersigned has received information that H. P. B., the outer Head of the Section, has departed this life; that the undersigned is going to London to confer upon the matter, and that until such conference is had all matters in the Section remain as they now are.

Upon my return, circulars will be sent to the Section as to its future conduct, and all members are requested to wait until then for that information, meanwhile continuing their work.

WILLIAM Q. JUDGE,
Secretary to H. P. B. in U. S.